THE 2026 GOTAXX STRATEGY
12 MONTHS TO TAX MASTERY

THE 2026 GOTAXX STRATEGY 12 MONTHS TO TAX MASTERY

TYRONE CAMPBELL

CONTENTS

Chapter ... vii

1	JANUARY: THE ULTIMATE TAX PREP KIT	1
6	FEBRUARY: CREDITS & DEDUCTIONS	17
11	MARCH: AUDIT-PROOFING YOUR FINANCES	33
16	APRIL: BEYOND THE REFUND	52
21	MAY: THE ENTREPRENEUR'S SPRING CLEANING	69
26	JUNE: MAJOR LIFE CHANGES & YOUR TAXES	86
31	JULY: THE MID-YEAR TAX CHECK-UP	102
36	AUGUST: EDUCATION, KIDS, AND THE IRS	119
41	SEPTEMBER: THE RETIREMENT ROADMAP	137
46	OCTOBER: REAL ESTATE STRATEGIES	153
51	NOVEMBER: THE ART OF GIVING	168
56	DECEMBER: THE YEAR-END COUNTDOWN	184

| 1 |

JANUARY: THE ULTIMATE TAX PREP KIT

THE MASTER DOCUMENT CHECKLIST

Eliminating "Document Drip" and Maximizing Accuracy

The most stressful part of tax season isn't usually the math—it's the "scavenger hunt." We call the habit of sending documents one by one as they arrive in the mail "Document Drip." Not only does this slow down your filing, but it also increases the risk of a missed deduction or a reporting error.

This chapter serves as your master inventory. Before you send a single file to our portal, ensure you have checked off every item in these three categories.

1. Income Streams: Where did your money come from?

The IRS receives a copy of every reporting form issued to you. To avoid a "matching notice" (and the penalties that come with it), we need to ensure our records match theirs exactly.

- **W-2s**: From every employer you worked for during 2025.
- **1099-NEC/MISC**: For any freelance work, "gig" economy jobs, or independent contracting.
- **1099-K**: If you received over the reporting threshold via Venmo, PayPal, or CashApp for business goods and services.
- **1099-INT & 1099-DIV**: From your bank accounts and brokerage firms for interest and dividends earned.
- **1099-B**: Summary of your stock or cryptocurrency sales (this is crucial for calculating capital gains/losses).
- **1099-R**: If you took a distribution from a retirement account or pension.

2. The "Deduction Trail": Lowering Your Bill

Deductions are "coupons" for your tax bill. If you don't have the documentation, we can't apply for the discount. Collect the following:

- **Form 1098 (Mortgage Interest)**: Sent by your lender; this often includes property taxes paid through escrow.
- **Property Taxes**: If not listed on your 1098, grab your most recent county tax statement.

- **Form 1098-E**: For any student loan interest paid during the year.
- **Charitable Receipts**: Written acknowledgments for cash donations over $250, and a detailed list/valuation for non-cash donations (like clothing or household goods).
- **Medical Expenses**: If you had significant out-of-pocket medical or dental costs that exceeded 7.5% of your income.

3. Personal Essentials: The Foundation

Even if we have worked together for years, confirming these details prevents identity errors that can lead to an immediate IRS rejection of your return.

- **Social Security Numbers:** Required for you, your spouse, and all dependents.
- **Direct Deposit Info**: A voided check or a clear screenshot of your bank routing and account numbers. (Note: Using direct deposit is the fastest way to receive a refund).
- **Last Year's Return**: If you are a new client, please provide a full copy of your 2024 tax return. This helps us spot "carry-forward" items that could save you money this year.

Pro-Tip: Create a physical or digital "Tax Bucket." As mail arrives throughout January, drop it in the bucket immediately. Do not open the envelope and leave the form on the counter! Wait until you have a "full house," then upload everything to us in one batch

| 2 |

THE WHAT'S NEW BRIEFING

Navigating the 2026 Policy Shifts

Tax laws are rarely static, but the 2026 season is particularly significant. Following the passage of the One Big Beautiful Bill (OBBB) Act, several provisions that were set to expire have been made permanent, while new credits and thresholds have been introduced to combat inflation.

In this briefing, we're highlighting the three biggest changes that will impact your bottom line this year.

1. New Thresholds: Protecting Your Income from "Bracket Creep"

Inflation can often push taxpayers into higher tax brackets even if their "real" purchasing power hasn't increased. To prevent this, the IRS has significantly expanded the tax brackets and increased the standard deduction for 2025 income (filed in 2026).

Standard Deduction Updates:

Filing Status	2025	2026 (New)
Single/Married Filing Single	$15,750	$16,100
Married Filing Joint	$31,500	$32,200
Head of Household	$23,625	$24,150

The "Senior Bonus": If you are age 65 or older, you may be eligible for an additional "bonus" deduction of up to $6,000 (individual) or $12,000 (joint), provided your income falls below certain thresholds ($75k single / $150k joint).

2. The 1099-K Reset: Digital Payment Rules

There has been a lot of confusion regarding apps like Venmo, PayPal, and CashApp. After several years of delays, the rules have been clarified.

- **The Threshold**: For the 2025 tax year, third-party platforms are generally not required to send a 1099-K unless you exceeded $20,000 in gross payments AND 200 transactions.
- **The "Taxable" Reality**: Just because you don't receive a form doesn't mean the income isn't taxable. If you sold goods or performed services for a profit, that income must be reported regardless of whether a 1099-K arrives in your mailbox.

3. Key Credit Boosts & Expiring Provisions

- **Child Tax Credit (CTC)**: The maximum credit has increased to $2,200 per qualifying child for this season.
- **SALT Deduction**: The cap for State and Local Tax deductions (SALT) has been temporarily increased to $40,000 for married couples filing jointly, though this is subject to income-based phase-outs.
- **Sunsetting Energy Credits**: Some residential energy-efficiency credits enacted in previous years have been accelerated for termination or reduced. If you made home improvements in 2025, we need to review those receipts immediately to ensure you don't miss the window.

The Expert Insight: These changes are generally taxpayer-friendly, but they require precise reporting. Our goal is to ensure you sit in the lowest possible bracket by utilizing these expanded thresholds effectively.

| 3 |

THE DIGITAL VAULT (ORGANIZING THE CHAOS)

Security, Speed, and the End of the Shoebox

In the past, tax season meant carrying a literal shoebox of receipts into an office. Today, that method isn't just slow—it's a security risk. Physical documents can be lost, and unencrypted email is a "playground" for identity thieves.

This chapter will show you how to use 2026's best tools to organize your data effortlessly and share it with us securely.

1. The Paperless Mindset: Scanning on the Go

The secret to a stress-free January is capturing documents in June. If you wait until tax time to scan a year's worth of receipts, you've already lost the battle. We recommend these two gold-standard tools for your smartphone:

- **Adobe Scan (Best for General Docs)**: It turns your phone into a high-powered PDF scanner. It automatically finds the edges of your document, removes shadows, and sharpens the text. It's perfect for W-2s, 1098s, and donation letters.
- **Expensify (Best for Business/Side Hustles)**: Their "SmartScan" technology doesn't just take a picture; it actually "reads" the receipt, extracting the merchant, date, and amount automatically. It even matches the receipt to your credit card transactions.

2. Secure File Sharing: Our Digital Front Door

Stop! Before you hit "Send" on that email... Standard email is like a postcard; anyone who handles it along the way can technically read it. Because your tax documents contain your Social Security Number and financial history, we strictly use a Secure Client Portal.

How to use our portal this year:

- **The One-Batch Rule**: While you can upload files as they come in, we recommend gathering everything in your "Digital Vault" first and then performing one bulk upload.
- **Mobile Uploads**: Our portal now allows you to snap a photo directly from your phone and upload it to your folder in seconds—no computer required.
- **Automatic Receipts**: Many of our clients now set up an "auto-forward" rule in their email for digital receipts (like Amazon Business or Uber), so they land in their tax folder without them ever lifting a finger.

3. Security First: Protecting Your Identity in 2026

Cyber-criminals have become more sophisticated, often using AI to create fake IRS "notices" or "urgent" texts about your refund.

- **The IRS Policy**: The IRS will never initiate contact with you via social media, text message, or email. Their primary method of contact is still the U.S. Postal Service.
- **Multi-Factor Authentication (MFA)**: We require MFA for our portal. This means that even if a hacker guesses your password, they cannot access your files without the one-time code sent to your phone. Always enable MFA on your bank and investment accounts as well.
- **Electronic-Only Refunds**: Starting this season, the IRS has moved toward an electronic-only refund model to prevent mail theft. Ensure your direct deposit information in our portal is 100% accurate to avoid delays.

The Peace of Mind Tip: Once a document is scanned and uploaded to our secure vault, it is backed up in the cloud. You no longer need to worry about fire, flood, or a misplaced folder ruining your records.

THE SMALL BUSINESS & SIDE HUSTLE PRIMER

Maximizing the Perks of Being Your Own Boss

For our self-employed clients and side-hustlers, tax season isn't just about reporting income—it's about recouping the costs of doing business. The One Big Beautiful Bill (OBBB) Act has introduced some of the most generous business incentives in a decade. This chapter covers the three "Heavy Hitters" of business deductions.

1. Home Office Reality Check: "Exclusive" is the Key

The Home Office deduction is one of the most misunderstood areas of the tax code. To qualify, your space must pass two strict IRS tests:

- **The Exclusive Use Test**: The area must be used only for business. A desk in the corner of your guest bedroom technically doesn't count if that room is also used for personal guests. A dedicated office, studio, or even a specific part of a room divided by a partition does.

- **The Principal Place of Business Test**: You must use the space regularly for administrative or management activities (billing, scheduling, client calls) and have no other fixed location where you conduct these tasks.

Which method should you choose?

- **The Simplified Method**: You claim $5 per square foot (up to 300 sq. ft.). This is the "no-headache" option that requires no tracking of utility bills.
- **The Regular Method**: We calculate the actual percentage of your home used for business and apply it to your rent/ mortgage interest, utilities, and insurance. If you live in a high-cost area, this almost always yields a bigger deduction.

2. Mileage Tracking: 70 Cents Adds Up Fast

For the 2025 tax year (filing in 2026), the IRS has increased the standard mileage rate to 70 cents per mile.

If you drive 5,000 miles for business, that is a $3,500 deduction. However, the IRS is aggressive about auditing mileage. A handwritten "guess" at the end of the year will not stand up.

- **The Digital Fix**: We strongly recommend using MileIQ or Everlance. These apps run in the background, log every drive via GPS, and allow you to swipe "Left" for personal and "Right" for business.

- **The Report**: At the end of the year, these apps generate a PDF log that meets every IRS record-keeping requirement. Simply upload that PDF to our portal.

3. Equipment & The "Section 179" Super-Deduction

Did you buy a new laptop, heavy machinery, or a business vehicle in 2025? Thanks to the OBBB Act, you may be able to deduct 100% of the purchase price in a single year rather than depreciating it over five to seven years.

- **The 2026 Limit**: You can now expense up to $2.5 million in qualifying equipment under Section 179.
- **Bonus Depreciation**: The OBBB Act also restored 100% Bonus Depreciation for 2025 purchases. This is a massive "win" for businesses looking to offset a high-income year with strategic spending.
- **The "Placed in Service" Rule**: To claim the deduction this year, you must have physically started using the equipment by December 31, 2025.

The Entrepreneur's Rule: If you aren't sure if an expense is "ordinary and necessary" for your business, save the receipt anyway. It's much easier for us to tell you "no" during our review than it is to hunt for a missing deduction after the deadline.

| 5 |

YOUR TAX SEASON TIMELINE

Deadlines, Myths, and the Early Bird Advantage

Timing is everything in the tax world. To ensure your return is filed accurately and your refund (if applicable) is processed quickly, you need to navigate several key dates. This chapter breaks down the 2026 calendar and debunks the most dangerous myth in tax preparation.

1. The 2026 Tax Calendar: Key Milestones

Mark these dates on your calendar. Missing them can lead to automatic penalties that are difficult to waive.

- **January 15, 2026**: Deadline for the final 2025 estimated tax payment.
- **January 31, 2026**: The "Mailing Deadline." This is the last day employers and financial institutions have to mail out your W-2s and 1099s.
  Note: Digital versions are often available a week earlier.

- **February 16, 2026 (Expected)**: The "Early Bird" window opens. This is typically when the IRS begins accepting and processing e-filed returns.
- **March 16, 2026**: The deadline for S-Corporations and Partnerships (Form 1120-S and 1065). If you own a business, your corporate return is due a full month before your personal one!
- **April 15, 2026**: Tax Day. This is the deadline for personal 1040 returns, C-Corporation returns, and the first estimated payment for 2026.

2. The "Early Bird" Window: Why February is Better

While you can wait until April, filing in February offers three distinct advantages:

- **Identity Theft Protection**: The sooner you file, the sooner your Social Security Number is "locked" in the IRS system for the year, preventing scammers from filing a fraudulent return in your name.
- **Faster Refunds**: The IRS typically processes early-season returns faster. Most e-filed returns with direct deposit are funded within 21 days.
- **Financial Clarity**: If you discover you owe money, filing in February gives you two full months to save up for the payment due on April 15th.

3. Debunking the Extension Myth

This is the most important takeaway of this guide: An extension to file is NOT an extension to pay.

If you file for an extension (Form 4868), the IRS gives you until October 15, 2026, to submit your paperwork. However, any taxes you owe for 2025 are still due in full by April 15, 2026.

- **The Penalty**: If you don't pay by April 15, the IRS will charge interest and a "failure to pay" penalty on the balance, even if you have a valid filing extension.
- **Our Policy**: If you need an extension, we must know by April 1st so we can help you estimate your tax liability and ensure your payment is sent on time.
- **The Professional Standard**: Our firm operates on a "first-in, first-out" basis. Clients who upload their completed Master Document Checklist by February 28th receive priority processing and the most dedicated time for strategic review.
- **Conclusion**: Your Path to a Stress-Free April

You've read the checklists, understood the new 2026 rules, and seen how digital tools can simplify your life. Now, there is only one step left: Putting the plan into motion.

Tax season doesn't have to be a sprint to the finish line. By starting now, you aren't just filing a return; you are protecting your wealth, securing your identity, and claiming back your time.

Step 1: Secure Your Spot

Our calendar fills up quickly, especially during the "Early Bird" February window. Don't wait for the April rush. Contact your tax preparer to choose a time for your initial consultation or document review.

Step 2: Pay It Forward

If you found this guide helpful, chances are your friends, family, or fellow business owners will too. We grow our firm through the trust of clients like you.

Simply share this e-book with them, or have them mention your name when they book their first appointment.

Final Reminder: The 3-Day Rule

Once you have collected all the items on your Master Document Checklist (Chapter 1), please upload them to the portal within 3 business days. This ensures we can maintain our turnaround promise and get your refund processed as fast as the IRS allows.

We look forward to making 2026 your most organized and profitable tax year yet!

| 6 |

FEBRUARY: CREDITS & DEDUCTIONS

THE GREAT DEBATE—STANDARD VS. ITEMIZED

Most taxpayers view the tax filing process as a chore to be completed, but for the savvy filer, it is actually a strategic decision-making process. The very first decision—and often the most consequential for your bottom line—is choosing between the Standard Deduction and Itemizing your deductions.

Think of this as the "fork in the road" of your tax return. Choosing the right path can be the difference between a modest refund and a significant windfall.

The Threshold: Knowing the Numbers

Every year, the IRS provides a "Standard Deduction"—a flat, no-questions-asked dollar amount that reduces your taxable income. You get this regardless of whether you spent a dime on deductible expenses.

For the 2025/2026 tax years, these thresholds have been adjusted for inflation, making the "hurdle" even higher for those who wish to itemize. If your total qualified expenses don't exceed these amounts, the Standard Deduction is your best friend. However, if your specific life expenses go just one dollar over these limits, you unlock the ability to reduce your taxable income even further.

Why it matters: If you are a married couple and your itemized expenses total $29,000, but the Standard Deduction is $30,000, taking the standard route saves you an extra $1,000 of taxable income. We always choose the path of least taxation.

When to Switch: The Itemization "Cheat Sheet"

When does it actually make sense to ignore the standard amount and list every expense on Schedule A? We generally look for three major "Heavy Hitters" that push our clients over the threshold:

- **High Mortgage Interest**: For many homeowners, especially those with newer or larger loans, the interest paid on a primary residence is the single largest factor in the decision to itemize.
- **Significant Medical Expenses**: If you had a year with major surgeries, dental work, or fertility treatments, you can deduct the portion of unreimbursed medical expenses that exceed 7.5% of your Adjusted Gross Income (AGI).
- **Large Charitable Gifts**: Generosity pays off. Whether it's cash to your church or donated goods to a local shelter, these

contributions can quickly bridge the gap to the itemization threshold.

- **State and Local Taxes (SALT)**: You can deduct up to $10,000 of your state and local income (or sales) taxes plus property taxes.

The "Bunching" Strategy: A Pro-Tip

What if you find yourself "stuck in the middle"—your expenses are high, but not quite high enough to beat the Standard Deduction? This is where we implement the Bunching Strategy.

Instead of giving a moderate amount to charity every year and receiving no tax benefit for it, you "bunch" two years of donations into one.

The Scenario:

- **Year 1**: You take the Standard Deduction and keep your charitable cash in a high-yield savings account.
- **Year 2**: In January, you make your usual donation. In December, you make your next year's donation early.

By stacking these expenses into a single tax year, you suddenly soar past the Standard Deduction threshold, allowing you to itemize and claim a much larger "Refund Boost" than you would have received otherwise

| 7 |

FAMILY & DEPENDENT CREDITS

THE BIG WINS

If Chapter 1 was about reducing the income the IRS can tax, Chapter 2 is about the "Heavy Hitters"—credits that wipe out your tax bill dollar-for-dollar. For families, these credits are often the largest single factor in a "Refund Boost." Thanks to recent legislation, many of these benefits have been expanded for the 2025 and 2026 tax years.

The Child Tax Credit (CTC): More Power per Child

The Child Tax Credit remains the "Gold Standard" of family tax breaks. For the 2025 tax year, the credit has increased to $2,200 per qualifying child (up from $2,000 in previous years).

- **Eligibility**: The child must be under age 17 at the end of the year, have a valid Social Security Number, and live with you for more than half the year.

- **Income Phase-Outs**: This credit isn't just for low-income families. You can claim the full credit as long as your Modified Adjusted Gross Income (MAGI) is below $400,000 for married couples or $200,000 for all other filers.
- **Refundability**: Even if you don't owe any tax, you may still receive up to $1,700 per child as a refund (known as the Additional Child Tax Credit).

Child and Dependent Care Credit: Getting Cash Back for Care

Many parents view daycare or summer camp as a necessary burden, but the IRS views it as a "work-related expense" that deserves a credit. If you pay for care so that you (and your spouse) can work or look for work, you likely qualify.

- What Counts: Daycare centers, private babysitters, after-school programs, and even summer day camps (overnight camps are excluded).
- The Limits: You can claim expenses up to $3,000 for one child or $6,000 for two or more children.
- The 2026 Upgrade: Under the new "One Big Beautiful Bill" provisions, the maximum credit rate is set to increase in 2026, allowing families to potentially recoup up to 50% of their care costs depending on income.

Pro-Tip: If your employer offers a Dependent Care Flexible Spending Account (FSA), you can often combine it with this credit for a "Double Dip" benefit—just remember you can't use the same expenses for both!

The "Other Dependent" Credit: Don't Forget the $500

A common mistake is assuming that once a child turns 17, the tax benefits stop. This is where the Credit for Other Dependents (ODC) comes in. This $500 non-refundable credit is designed for:

1. **High Schoolers & College Students**: Children age 17–23 who are full-time students.
2. **Aging Parents**: If you provide more than half the support for a parent or elderly relative, even if they don't live with you, you may be eligible.
3. **Extended Family**: Aunts, uncles, or even "qualifying relatives" who live in your home all year and earn less than the IRS income limit (roughly $5,200 for 2025).

While $500 may seem small compared to the CTC, it is a permanent fixture of the tax code that many taxpayers leave on the table simply because they didn't check a box.

| 8 |

EDUCATION & STUDENT SAVINGS

Education Tax Credits

Education is often one of a family's largest investments, but the tax code offers several ways to "reimburse" you for those costs. Whether you are paying for your child's first year of college, finishing your own master's degree, or finally paying off those student loans, there is likely a "Refund Booster" waiting for you.

The American Opportunity Tax Credit (AOTC): The $2,500 Win

The AOTC is specifically designed for students in their first four years of post-secondary education. It is generally the most valuable education credit because it is partially refundable.

- **The Math:** You can claim 100% of the first $2,000 spent on tuition, fees, and required equipment (like books or a laptop), plus 25% of the next $2,000. This adds up to a maximum credit of $2,500 per student, per year.

- **The Refundable Edge**: Even if your tax bill is zero, you can receive up to $1,000 (40% of the credit) as a refund.
- **The Rules**: The student must be enrolled at least half-time in a program leading to a degree or certificate. Note that the full credit begins to phase out for single filers earning over $80,000 (or $160,000 for married couples filing jointly).

Lifetime Learning Credit (LLC): Flexibility for Every Stage

If the AOTC is the "undergrad" credit, the LLC is for everyone else. It is perfect for grad students, professional development, or even a single course taken to improve job skills.

- **The Benefit**: It provides a credit of up to $2,000 per tax return (calculated as 20% of the first $10,000 of qualified expenses).
- **No "Four-Year" Limit**: Unlike the AOTC, which cuts off after four years, you can claim the LLC for an unlimited number of years.
- **Key Differences**: The LLC is non-refundable (it can only bring your tax bill to zero) and it does not require the student to be in a degree program or enrolled half-time.

Planning Tip: You can claim the AOTC for one child and the LLC for another (or yourself) on the same tax return, but you cannot claim both credits for the same student in the same year.

Student Loan Interest: An "Above-the-Line" Save

If you are still paying off education from years ago, you haven't been forgotten. The IRS allows you to deduct up to $2,500 in student loan interest paid during the year.

- **No Itemizing Required**: This is an "above-the-line" deduction, meaning you get to take it even if you chose the Standard Deduction in Chapter 1. It directly reduces your Adjusted Gross Income (AGI).
- **The Income Test**: For the 2025 tax year, the ability to take this deduction begins to phase out for single filers at $85,000 of income and for married couples at $170,000.
- **Who Can Claim It**: You must be legally obligated to pay the loan, and you cannot be claimed as a dependent on someone else's return.

| 9 |

THE HIDDEN GEMS

OFTEN OVERLOOKED

While the major credits for families and students get most of the spotlight, the tax code is filled with "Hidden Gems"—smaller, specialized provisions that can collectively save you thousands. These are the items that often separate a standard filing from a high-level tax plan.

Energy-Efficient Home Credits: The $3,200 Annual Reset

Under the Inflation Reduction Act, the tax benefits for going green have been supercharged. Unlike the old "lifetime" limits, the Energy Efficient Home Improvement Credit now resets every single year through 2025.

- **The 30% Rule**: You can claim a credit for 30% of the cost of qualified upgrades.
- **The $1,200 General Limit**: This covers weatherization like new exterior doors ($250 per door, $500 max), windows

and skylights ($600 max), and professional home energy audits ($150).

- **The $2,000 "Bonus" Limit**: If you install a qualified heat pump, heat pump water heater, or biomass stove, you can claim an additional $2,000 credit.
- **Total Potential**: By timing your upgrades correctly, you could claim up to $3,200 in credits every year until the current provisions expire at the end of 2025.

Educator Expenses: A Thank You to K-12 Teachers

Teachers are famous for spending their own money to keep their classrooms running. The IRS offers a small but vital "above-the-line" deduction to help recoup those costs.

- **The 2025 Limit**: Eligible educators can deduct up to $300 for books, supplies, computer equipment, and even supplementary materials.
- **The "Double" Benefit**: If you are married and both spouses are educators, you can deduct up to $600 on a joint return.
- **The 2026 Shift**: Under the newly passed "One Big Beautiful Bill" (OBBBA), the 2026 tax year will see this limit increase to $350 above-the-line, with additional expenses potentially becoming itemized deductions for those who qualify.
- **Health Savings Accounts (HSA)**: The "Triple-Tax Advantage"

If you have a High-Deductible Health Plan (HDHP), the HSA is perhaps the most powerful wealth-building tool in the tax code. It is often called a "Stealth IRA" because:

1. Contributions are 100% tax-deductible (reducing your income).
2. Growth is tax-free (you pay no tax on capital gains or interest).
3. Withdrawals are tax-free (as long as they are used for medical expenses).

For 2025, you can contribute up to $4,300 for individuals or $8,550 for families. If you are 55 or older, you can add an extra $1,000 "catch-up" contribution.

Jury Duty Pay: Don't Pay Tax on Money You Didn't Keep

This is a classic "Hidden Gem" that many people miss. If you served on a jury and your employer continued to pay your full salary, they likely required you to "hand over" your jury duty pay from the court to the company.

- **The Problem**: The court will still issue you a 1099 or report that pay as income to the IRS.
- **The Fix**: You must report that jury pay as income, but you are allowed to take an equal deduction for the amount you gave to your employer. This ensures you aren't paying income tax on money that effectively went straight to your boss.

| 10 |

AVOIDING THE RED FLAGS

The Real Victory

Getting a larger refund is a victory, but the goal is to keep that money—not hand it back later with interest and penalties. The IRS has significantly increased its enforcement capabilities for the 2025 and 2026 tax years, using AI-driven "matching" programs to spot inconsistencies in seconds.

To protect your "Refund Boost," you need to know what triggers an audit and how to document your way out of one.
The "Too Good to Be True" Trap: Social Media Scams

In 2025, the IRS placed "Social Media Tax Advice" on its official "Dirty Dozen" list of tax scams. You should be extremely wary of "tax influencers" on TikTok or Instagram promising "secret" loopholes. Common red flags include:

- The "Fuel Tax Credit" Scam: Promoters claiming that everyday drivers can claim credits meant for off-highway business equipment (like farm tractors).

- Fictional Business Expenses: Advice to "write off your life" by claiming personal groceries, gym memberships, or family vacations as business costs.
- Clean Energy Overstatements: Claiming the full $3,200 energy credit for minor repairs that don't meet the strict efficiency standards of the Inflation Reduction Act.

Reasonableness: The "Ordinary & Necessary" Test

When it comes to business deductions (Schedule C) or unreimbursed expenses, the IRS uses a scoring system called DIF (Discriminant Function System). It compares your deductions to the "norms" for your income and profession.

- The Audit Trigger: If you earn $100,000 but claim $40,000 in "Travel and Meals," your return will likely be flagged for a manual review.
- Business Meals: For 2025, business meals remain 50% deductible, but they must be "ordinary and necessary." You must be able to prove who you were with and what business was discussed.
- The 2026 Cliff: Be aware that under current 2026 guidelines, many "de minimis" meal deductions (like office snacks) are scheduled to drop to 0% deductibility unless they are tied to specific travel or holiday parties.

The Importance of Proof: Your Paper Trail

If the IRS asks for proof, "I forgot" is not a legal defense. Digital records are your best friend. For 2025, the IRS accepts digital scans and photos of receipts as long as they are legible.

Expense Type	What to Keep	How Long?
Standard Deductions	W-2s, 1099s, 1098-T (Education)	3-7 Years
Charitable Gifts	Receipts (if >$250) or bank statements	7 Years
Home Improvements	Invoices & efficiency certifications	7 Years after sale
Business Mileage	A log showing Date, Miles, and Purpose	3 Years

Pro-Tip: The "Safe Zone" for most taxpayers is seven years. While the standard audit window is three years, the IRS can look back six years if they believe you underreported your income by more than 25%.

CONCLUSION & CALL TO ACTION (CTA)

Tax laws are not written in stone; they are a moving target. As we move through 2025 and into the major shifts of 2026, the difference between a "standard" return and a "maximized" return comes down to planning, not just preparation.

The "Review My Returns" Offer

Not sure if you missed something last year? Tax laws changed significantly mid-season, and many taxpayers left money on the table. We offer a Look-Back Service where we review your previous three years of filings. If we find unclaimed credits (like the

AOTC or Energy credits) that you qualified for, we can file an amendment to get that money back in your pocket.

Schedule Your Session

Don't wait until April 14th to start thinking about these "Boosters." The best strategies—like Bunching or HSA contributions—must be executed before the year ends.

| 11 |

MARCH: AUDIT-PROOFING YOUR FINANCES

UNDERSTANDING THE RED FLAGS

Why the IRS Computer Cries "Foul"

Most people imagine an IRS audit as a stern man in a suit knocking on their front door. In reality, modern "audits" usually begin in a data center. The IRS uses a sophisticated computer system called the Discriminant Inventory Function (DIF). This system scores every return based on "norms" for your income level and profession.

If your "score" is too high, a human agent takes a look. To keep your score low, you need to understand the three primary triggers that set off the automated alarms.

1. The Matching Game: The CP2000 Trap

The IRS is a giant data-matching machine. For every W-2, 1099, or 1098 you receive, the IRS receives a carbon copy. If you forget to report even a tiny amount of income—like $12 in interest from an old savings account—the computer identifies a "mismatch."

This triggers a CP2000 Notice. While not a full audit, it is an automated bill for the tax on the missing income, plus interest.

- **The Lesson**: Never guess your income. Wait for every single form to arrive before we file. Even a "negligible" amount of missing income tells the IRS computer that the rest of your return might be unreliable.

2. The Danger of "Perfect" Numbers

In the world of real business, numbers are messy. You pay $42.87 for gas, $119.20 for a utility bill, and $1,204.55 for insurance. When the IRS sees a tax return filled with perfectly rounded numbers—$500 for office supplies, $1,000 for travel, $200 for meals—it sends a signal that you are estimating rather than calculating.

- **The Lesson**: Precision is your best defense. Reporting exactly $487.62 shows the IRS that you are looking at a receipt or a bank statement. Reporting $500 shows them you are guessing. The IRS hates guesses.

3. Lifestyle vs. Income (The "Smell Test")

The IRS knows the average cost of living in your zip code. If you report an adjusted gross income of $30,000 but claim $25,000 in itemized deductions—including heavy costs for a luxury vehicle or a high-value mortgage—the computer flags a "Reasonableness" error.

The IRS's logic is simple: How are you paying for your life? If your business expenses and deductions leave you with no money to pay for basic groceries and housing, they will suspect "under-reported income."

- **The Lesson**: Your tax return should tell a logical story. If you had a lean year but high expenses, we need to ensure your documentation explains why (such as using savings or a business loan) to justify the lifestyle-to-income gap.

Summary Checklist for Chapter 1:

- **Gather all 1099s**: Even the ones for tiny amounts
- **Avoid Rounding**: Use the exact cents from your records.
- **The Reality Check**: Ensure your reported profit can reasonably support your cost of living.

| 12 |

THE HOME OFFICE & TRAVEL

DANGER ZONES

If Chapter 11 was about the "eyes" of the IRS computer, Chapter 12 is about the "magnifying glass." Certain deductions are known as "Super-Red Flags" because they are frequently abused. To the IRS, the Home Office and Business Vehicle deductions are like low-hanging fruit—if you aren't following the rules to the letter, they are very easy to pluck away.

1. The "Exclusive Use" Rule

The Home Office deduction is one of the most misunderstood areas of tax law. Many taxpayers believe that if they answer emails at the kitchen table, they have a home office.

The IRS strictly enforces the "Exclusive Use" test. This means the area you claim must be used only for business.

- The Kitchen Table Test: If your children eat cereal at the same table where you do your bookkeeping, it is not a home office.
- The Guest Room Test: If your office contains a bed where your mother-in-law sleeps once a year, it is not exclusive use.

Pro-Tip: Take a photo of your dedicated office space. If you are ever questioned, a single timestamped photo showing a desk, computer, and filing cabinet in a distinct area is worth a thousand words.

2. The 100% Business Vehicle Myth

This is perhaps the single most common trigger for a manual audit. If you tell the IRS that your primary vehicle is used 100% for business, they will almost certainly investigate.

Unless you own a specialized vehicle (like a branded delivery van or a heavy-duty crane) that stays at a job site, the IRS assumes you use your car to go to the grocery store, the gym, or a doctor's appointment at least once in a while.

- The Commuting Rule: Driving from your home to your first place of work is considered "commuting," which is not deductible.

- The Solution: Keep a mileage log. Whether it's an app (like MileIQ) or a physical notebook in the glove box, you must track:
    - 1. The date
    - 2. The mileage
    - 3. The business purpose (e.g., "Meeting with client at 123 Main St")

3. Meal & Entertainment Reality

The rules for business dining have shifted significantly in recent years. Many taxpayers are still trying to deduct "Entertainment"—like golf outings or concert tickets—which are generally no longer deductible.

Current rules focus on Business Meals. To be deductible:

- The taxpayer (or an employee) must be present.
- The meal cannot be "lavish or extravagant."
- You must have a clear business discussion before, during, or after the meal.
- **The Lesson**: On every meal receipt, quickly jot down who you were with and what was discussed. "Dinner with Sarah J. re: Q3 Marketing Strategy" is audit-proof. A blank receipt for $150 at a steakhouse is a target.

Summary Checklist for Chapter 12:

- Measure your office: Know the exact square footage of your exclusive workspace.
- Download a mileage app: Start tracking today; don't wait until December to "reconstruct" your year.
- Audit your receipts: Make sure your dining receipts include the names of the people present.

DOCUMENTATION–YOUR FINANCIAL ARMOR

Proof and Support

In the tax world, there is a legal concept that surprises most people: The Burden of Proof. In a criminal court, you are innocent until proven guilty. But in a tax audit, the IRS assumes their assessment is correct until you prove otherwise.

Without documentation, you aren't just "unorganized"—you are defenseless. This chapter will show you how to build a suit of financial armor that makes you virtually "un-auditable."

1. The Burden of Proof: Why "I Think" Doesn't Count

When we claim a deduction on your tax return, we are making a legal assertion. If the IRS asks for proof, a bank statement showing a withdrawal isn't enough. Why? Because a $200 withdrawal from an ATM could be for printer ink (deductible) or for a nice dinner with your spouse (not deductible).

To meet the burden of proof, you need Substantiation. This means having:

- **The Receipt**: To show what was bought.
- **The Context**: To show why it was for business.

The Golden Rule: If you can't prove it, you can't deduct it. Our goal is to ensure that for every line on your tax return, there is a corresponding digital or physical folder ready to back it up.

2. The 7-Year Rule (and the Truth About 3 Years)

You may have heard that the IRS only has 3 years to audit you. While that is the standard "statute of limitations," there are major exceptions:

- **The 6-Year Rule**: If you under-report your income by more than 25%, the IRS can look back six years.
- **The 7-Year Rule**: If you claim a loss from worthless securities or bad debt deductions, you must keep records for seven years.
- **The "Forever" Rule**: If you fail to file a return or file a fraudulent one, there is no time limit.

Our Recommendation: Keep everything for 7 years. It's a clean, safe standard that covers all bases.

3. Digital vs. Paper: What Does the IRS Accept?

The good news? The IRS has been fully digital since 1997. You do not need to keep shoeboxes of fading thermal paper receipts.

Requirements for Digital Records:

1. **Legible**: If you can't read the scan, the IRS won't accept it.
2. **Identifiable**: The digital copy must exhibit a high degree of legibility and be able to be reproduced.
3. **Complete**: You should scan both sides of a document if there is relevant information on the back.

The Best Practice: Use a "Scan-and-Shred" workflow. Use an app to snap a photo of a receipt the moment you get it, upload it to a cloud folder (organized by year and category), and toss the paper.

4. The Logbook Habit: Your Best Defense

For certain "listed property" like vehicles, a receipt isn't enough. The IRS specifically looks for a Contemporaneous Log.

"Contemporaneous" is a fancy way of saying "recorded at the time of the event."

Trying to recreate a mileage log in April for a trip you took last June is nearly impossible and looks suspicious to an auditor.

- The Calendar Method: Your digital calendar (Google or Outlook) is a powerful piece of evidence. If you have an entry for "Meeting with Client X" and a corresponding mileage entry, your defense is rock solid.

Summary Checklist for Chapter 3:

- The 7-Year Purge: Shred anything older than 7 years, but keep everything else.
- Go Digital: Start using a cloud-based storage system (Dropbox, Google Drive, or our firm's secure portal).
- Note the "Why": For any expense over $75, ensure the business purpose is documented.

| 14 |

THE CRYPTO & DIGITAL ASSET TRAP

New Crypto Reporting

If you've dipped your toes into Bitcoin, Ethereum, or even a local NFT project, you are now a high-priority interest for the IRS. For years, the digital asset world was the "Wild West"—but in 2025, the sheriff has officially arrived. The IRS has overhauled its systems specifically to capture every pixel of digital profit.

1. The Mandatory Question

Every taxpayer filing a Form 1040 is now met with a front-and-center question: "At any time during 2024/2025, did you receive, sell, exchange, or otherwise dispose of a digital asset?"

This is not a suggestion; it is a legal requirement to answer "Yes" or "No."

- **The Perjury Trap**: If you check "No" while holding a Coinbase or Kraken account that saw activity, you aren't just making a mistake—you are technically signing a fraudulent return.
- **The "Holding" Exception**: If you simply bought Bitcoin with USD and it sat in your wallet all year without being sold or traded, you can safely answer "No."

2. The Exchange Trap: Why "Cashing Out" Isn't the Only Trigger

The most common myth in crypto is: "I don't owe taxes until I move the money back to my bank account." This is false.
The IRS views a crypto-to-crypto trade (e.g., swapping Bitcoin for Ethereum) as a taxable event. You are essentially "selling" one property to "buy" another.

- Stablecoins count too: Even swapping a volatile coin for a stablecoin like USDC is a disposal that triggers a gain or loss.
- New in 2025 (Form 1099-DA): Beginning in 2025, crypto brokers and exchanges are required to issue Form 1099-DA. Just like a 1099-B from an E*TRADE account, the IRS will receive a copy of your digital asset proceeds. The "Matching Game" we discussed in

Chapter 14 now applies to your crypto wallets.

3. The New "Wallet-by-Wallet" Rule

In 2025, the IRS introduced a major technical shift. Previously, investors could use "universal" accounting to track their costs across all accounts. Now, the IRS requires wallet-by-wallet cost tracking.

This means you must track the "basis" (what you paid) for the specific assets in each individual wallet or exchange. If you transfer assets between wallets, the paperwork must follow.

4. Tracking Software: Your Digital Paper Trail

Trying to track hundreds of trades across three different exchanges and a hardware wallet using an Excel sheet is a recipe for an audit. Because of the new 1099-DA requirements and wallet-specific rules, professional tracking software is no longer "optional" for active traders.

Recommended Tools:

- **CoinLedger or Koinly**: Excellent for generating IRS-ready reports that sync directly with our professional tax software.
- **ZenLedger**: Great for those with complex DeFi (Decentralized Finance) or NFT activity.
- **The Professional Shield**: If you use these tools, we can import a "Tax Loss Harvesting" report. This doesn't just keep you safe—it helps us find ways to use your crypto losses to offset your other income, potentially saving you thousands.

Summary Checklist for Chapter 14:

- **Audit your Wallets**: Make a list of every exchange (Coinbase, Binance) and every "cold" wallet (Ledger, MetaMask) you used this year.
- **Identify "Swaps"**: Remember that trading one coin for another is a sale in the eyes of the IRS.
- **Sync Early**: Don't wait until April 14th to sync your crypto software; API errors and missing data take time to fix.

| 15 |

I GOT A LETTER... NOW WHAT?

Don't Ignore That notice

Even if you follow every rule in this playbook, you may still receive a letter from the IRS. It's important to remember: A letter is not a conviction. It is the beginning of a conversation. How you handle the first 30 days of that conversation will determine whether the issue is resolved quickly or turns into a multi-year headache.

1. The Correspondence Audit: The Most Likely Scenario

As we've discussed, most "audits" today are actually Correspondence Examinations. These are conducted entirely by mail and usually focus on just one or two specific items.

- **The Request**: They might ask for a specific receipt for a charitable donation or a copy of your 1099-B from a brokerage.

- **The Mistake**: Many people panic and send everything they have for the entire year.
- **The Strategy**: Only send exactly what is requested. Over-sharing can give an auditor a reason to expand the scope of their inquiry into other parts of your return.

2. The 30-Day Clock: Your Most Important Deadline

IRS letters are time-sensitive. Most notices give you exactly 30 days from the date on the letter (not the date you received it) to respond.

What happens if you ignore the clock?

1. **Loss of Rights**: You may lose the right to challenge the IRS's findings in Appeals.
2. **Automated Billing**: The IRS computer will assume their proposed "adjustment" is correct and will automatically issue a bill for the tax, plus penalties and interest.
3. **The "90-Day Letter"**: If you ignore the 30-day notice, you'll receive a "Statutory Notice of Deficiency." At this point, your only way to fight the bill is to file a petition in U.S. Tax Court.

Rule of Thumb: As soon as you see an IRS logo in your mailbox, open it and check the date. If you are traveling or away, have someone check your mail. The IRS does not accept "I was on vacation" as a valid excuse for missing a deadline.

3. The Professional Shield: Don't Face the IRS Alone

One of the most valuable rights you have as a taxpayer is the Right to Representation. This means you can authorize a professional (like our firm) to stand between you and the IRS.

Why you should never call the IRS yourself:

- **The "Nervous Slip"**: Taxpayers often offer more information than necessary out of nervousness. An auditor is trained to listen for "leads" that can justify expanding the audit.
- **Interpreting the Law**: You might know your business, but a professional knows the Internal Revenue Code. We speak "IRS language" and can often shut down a line of questioning by citing the specific tax law that applies to your situation.
- **The Buffer Zone**: When we represent you, you usually don't even have to speak to the auditor. We handle the phone calls, the document uploads, and the negotiations. This allows you to focus on your life and business while we handle the "Boogeyman."

Summary Checklist for Chapter 5:

- **Don't Panic**: Read the letter carefully to identify the "Letter Number" in the top right corner.
- **Watch the Calendar**: Mark the 30-day deadline the moment you open the envelope.

- **Call the Pros**: Send us a copy of the letter immediately. We will review it and determine if it's a simple fix or requires a formal defense.

| 16 |

APRIL: BEYOND THE REFUND

THE PSYCHOLOGY OF THE REFUND

For most Americans, tax season ends with a sigh of relief and a specific, highly anticipated number: the refund. We've been conditioned to view that check from the IRS as a "bonus" or a "windfall." It feels like "found money"—a gift from the government for successfully navigating the labyrinth of tax forms. But if you want to move beyond the cycle of living paycheck to paycheck and start building true, generational wealth, we have to dismantle that myth.

To change your financial future, you must first change how you feel about your refund.

The "Interest-Free Loan" Reality

Imagine if a friend approached you and asked to borrow $5,000. You agree, but with one condition: they won't pay you back for twelve months, and when they do, they won't pay you a single cent in interest.

You would likely call that a bad deal. Yet, this is exactly what happens when you receive a large tax refund.

A refund isn't a gift; it is an overpayment. It is money that you earned through your hard work that was withheld from your paycheck and sent to the IRS. By over-withholding, you have essentially given the federal government an interest-free loan for an entire year. While that money was sitting in the government's coffers, it wasn't working for you. It wasn't earning interest in a high-yield savings account, it wasn't growing in the stock market, and it wasn't helping you pay down debt.

The Forced Savings Trap

Many people argue that a large refund is the only way they can save money. They call it "forced savings." They worry that if they had that extra $400 in their monthly paycheck instead of getting it back in April, they would just "blow it" on coffee or dinners out.

This is the Forced Savings Trap. While it feels safe, it is mathematically inefficient for two reasons:

1. **Opportunity Cost**: If you receive a $4,800 refund in April, you missed out on 12 months of potential growth. If that $400 per month had been diverted into an investment ac-

count, you would have the principal plus the compound interest.

2. **Inflation**: In an inflationary environment, a dollar today is worth more than a dollar a year from now. By letting the IRS hold your money, you are getting paid back in "cheaper" dollars that have less purchasing power than when you earned them.

Wealthy individuals don't "force" savings through the IRS. They automate savings through their own accounts.

Smart Spending vs. Strategic Investing

When a refund check hits your bank account, the "dopamine hit" is real. It's tempting to treat it as "fun money"—a new television, a weekend getaway, or a luxury purchase.

However, the psychological shift happens when you stop viewing the refund as a "spending budget" and start viewing it as a "wealth catalyst." Consider the difference in impact:

- **The Splurge**: You spend a $5,000 refund on a vacation. The memories are great, but the money is gone forever.
- **The Catalyst**: You put that $5,000 into a diversified index fund. At a 7% average annual return, that single "refund" could grow to nearly $20,000 in 20 years without you adding another dime.

The Bottom Line: Your refund is the first test of your financial discipline for the new year. Are you going to give the government another interest-free loan next year, or are you ready to take control of your cash flow today?

| 17 |

THE W-4 PAYCHECK TUNE-UP

Too Much or Too Little

Once you've shifted your mindset and realized that a massive refund is actually a missed opportunity, the next logical question is: How do I stop it? The answer lies in a simple, often overlooked document—the IRS Form W-4.

Most people fill out a W-4 on their first day of work and never look at it again. However, this form is the "control dial" for your monthly wealth building. If your dial is set too high, the government takes too much; if it's set too low, you'll face a surprise bill in April. Our goal is to find the "Sweet Spot."

Finding the Sweet Spot

The "Sweet Spot" is the point where you owe $0 and get $0 back at the end of the year. While that might not sound as exciting as a $5,000 check, look at what it actually achieves: it maximizes your monthly cash flow.

By adjusting your withholdings to match your actual tax liability, you are essentially giving yourself an immediate raise. Instead of waiting for the IRS to "approve" your access to your own money in April, you get that money on the 1st and 15th of every month.

The "Pay Yourself First" Strategy

The biggest fear people have when they reduce their withholding is that they will spend the extra money on trivial things. To avoid this, you must treat your W-4 adjustment like a subscription to your future.

The moment your "Paycheck Tune-Up" takes effect, you should implement the "Pay Yourself First" rule. Here is how to do it:

1. Calculate the Difference: If your paycheck increases by $400 due to your W-4 change, that is your "wealth-building seed."
2. Automate the Transfer: Set up an automatic transfer from your checking account to a High-Yield Savings Account (HYSA) or a brokerage account.
3. Sync the Dates: Schedule the transfer for the same day your direct deposit hits.

By doing this, the money is gone before you even have a chance to miss it. You have effectively created your own "forced savings" plan, but with one massive advantage: you keep the interest.

Why It Matters for Your Financial Future

When you control your cash flow, you gain agility. * In an emergency: You have extra cash every month to handle a flat tire or a broken appliance without reaching for a credit card.

- In a market dip: You have consistent capital to invest when prices are low, rather than waiting for a refund that might arrive after the market has already recovered.

Adjusting your W-4 isn't just a clerical task; it's a declaration that you are the CFO of your own life. You are taking back the steering wheel from the IRS and putting your money to work the moment it's earned.

| 18 |

TAX-EFFICIENT INVESTING 101

Thinking about Retirement

Now that you've reclaimed your monthly cash flow by tuning up your W-4, the next question is: **Where should that money live?** Not all investment accounts are created equal. In the world of wealth building, it's not just about what you earn; it's about how much you keep after the IRS takes its cut. This is the art of tax-efficient investing. By understanding where to place your assets, you can significantly accelerate your path to financial freedom.

Asset Location: The "Tax-Free" vs. "Tax-Deferred" Map

Think of your investment accounts like different types of buckets. Some buckets protect your money from taxes now, while others protect it later.

- **The Roth IRA/401(k) (Tax-Free Growth):** This is the holy grail of accounts. You contribute money that has already been taxed, but from that point on, the money grows tax-free, and you pay $0 in taxes when you withdraw it in retirement.

- **The Standard Brokerage Account**: This bucket is flexible—you can take the money out whenever you want. However, you will pay taxes on the dividends you earn and the capital gains when you sell.
- **The Traditional IRA/401(k) (Tax-Deferred)**: You get a tax break today, but you'll owe the IRS their share when you retire and start taking the money out.

The Strategy: High-growth assets (like stocks) are often best suited for Roth accounts, where their massive growth can never be taxed.

The Power of the HSA: The "Triple Threat"

If there is a "secret weapon" in the tax code, it is the Health Savings Account (HSA). Most people think of it as a way to pay for doctor visits, but the wealthy use it as a powerful investment vehicle. It offers a Triple Tax Advantage:

1. **Tax-Deductible In**: Every dollar you put in lowers your taxable income for the year.
2. **Tax-Free Growth**: Your investments inside the HSA grow without being taxed.
3. **Tax-Free Out**: As long as you use the money for qualified medical expenses, you never pay taxes on the withdrawal.

Pro-Tip: If you can afford to pay for your current medical out-of-pocket, leave the money in the HSA to grow. Save your receipts; you can reimburse yourself years—or even decades—later using that tax-free growth.

Capital Gains Awareness: Timing is Everything

When you do invest in a standard brokerage account, the IRS rewards patience.

- **Short-Term Capital Gains**: If you sell an investment you've held for less than a year, the profit is taxed at your regular income tax rate (which can be as high as 37%).
- **Long-Term Capital Gains**: If you hold for at least one year and one day, that tax rate drops significantly—for many, it's only 15%.

Simply waiting 366 days to sell an asset can save you thousands of dollars in taxes. Wealthy investors don't just look at the stock price; they look at the calendar.

Key Takeaway: Tax efficiency is about playing the "long game." By choosing the right accounts and holding assets longer, you ensure that the growth of your wealth stays in your pocket, not the government's.

| 19 |

DEBT VS. INVESTMENT—THE GREAT DEBATE

Financial Fork in the Road

When that tax refund (or your newly increased monthly cash flow) hits your bank account, you face one of the most common dilemmas in personal finance: Do I pay off what I owe, or do I invest for what I want?

There is no one-size-fits-all answer, but there is a logical framework you can use to make the "right" decision for your specific situation. It comes down to two factors: Mathematical ROI and Psychological ROI.

The Interest Rate Math: The "6% Rule"

To make a logical choice, you have to compare the "guaranteed" return of paying off debt against the "expected" return of the stock market.

A helpful heuristic used by many financial experts is the 6% Rule:

- **High-Interest Debt (Above 6%)**: This includes credit cards (often 20%+) and personal loans. Paying these off is a guaranteed return on your money. If you have a credit card at 24% interest, paying it off is mathematically equivalent to finding an investment that pays a guaranteed 24% return—something that doesn't exist in the open market. Prioritize this first.
- **Low-Interest Debt (Below 6%)**: This often includes older mortgages or subsidized student loans. If your mortgage is at 3.5%, but the S&P 500 has historically averaged around 10% (before inflation), the math suggests you are better off investing the extra cash. You are "arbitraging" the difference—paying 3.5% to potentially earn 10%.

Emergency Fund First: Your Financial Armor

Before you put a single dollar into the S&P 500 or make an extra payment on your mortgage, you must check your "armor." In the financial world, that armor is your Emergency Fund.

Financial planners generally recommend having 3 to 6 months of essential living expenses in a liquid, high-yield savings account.

- **Why it's the priority**: Without an emergency fund, a sudden job loss or medical bill will force you back into high-interest debt (credit cards), undoing all your hard work.
- **The Refund Strategy**: Your tax refund is the perfect "seed money" to jumpstart this fund. If you don't have $1,000 in the bank for a rainy day, your refund shouldn't go to the

stock market or the mortgage—it should go to your peace of mind.

The "Mental ROI": Peace of Mind vs. Spreadsheets

While the math might say, "Don't pay off that 3% mortgage," the human brain doesn't always live in a spreadsheet.

For many, the psychological weight of debt causes stress that no 7% market gain can offset. This is what we call Mental ROI. If being completely debt-free allows you to sleep better at night, that has a value that isn't captured in a compound interest formula.

The Balanced Approach: If you're torn, split the difference. Use 50% of your extra funds to attack debt and 50% to build your investment portfolio. You get the mathematical benefit of time in the market and the psychological win of seeing your liabilities shrink.

SETTING YOUR TAX-FREE GOALS FOR NEXT YEAR

Building Wealth Past Tax Season

Wealth isn't built in the weeks leading up to April 15th; it is built in the 365 days that follow it. To move from being a "taxpayer" to a "wealth builder," you need a proactive roadmap. In this final chapter, we will establish a 12-month calendar for your money and explore the advanced tools that high-income earners use to shield their growth from the IRS.

The Calendar of Savings: A 12-Month Plan

Most people treat their finances like a series of emergencies. A "wealth builder" treats them like a schedule. Here is how to structure your year:

- **January – February**: The "Look Back." Review your previous year's earnings and adjust your W-4 based on the refund (or bill) you expect. Maximize any remaining contributions for the previous tax year (you have until April 15th for IRAs and HSAs).

- **April 15**: The "Pivot." Instead of celebrating a refund, celebrate the fact that your new monthly automation is already 3 months deep.
- **July**: The "Mid-Year Check." Are you on track to hit your 401(k) or IRA limits? For 2025, the employee contribution limit for a 401(k) is $23,500. If you aren't on pace, increase your percentage now.
- **October – November**: The "Tax Loss Harvesting" window. Review your brokerage accounts. If you have "losers" (investments that went down), you can sell them to offset the gains from your "winners," reducing your total tax bill.
- **December 31**: The "Finish Line." Ensure all 401(k) contributions are completed, as these generally must be made by year-end (unlike IRAs).

Advanced Tools: The "Mega-Backdoor" and More

If you are a high-income earner, you may find that you "max out" the standard retirement accounts quickly. This is where advanced strategies come into play:

1. The Mega-Backdoor Roth

This is the "heavy lifting" tool of tax planning. While a standard Roth IRA limits you to $7,000 per year (for 2025), the Mega-Backdoor Roth allows some employees to move up to an additional $46,500 into a tax-free Roth environment.

- How it works: If your employer's 401(k) plan allows "after-tax contributions" (distinct from Roth or Pre-tax) and "in-plan conversions," you can contribute up to the total limit of $70,000 (including employer matches) and immediately convert the excess into a Roth.

2. The Backdoor Roth IRA

If your income is too high to contribute directly to a Roth IRA (the phase-out starts at $150,000 for singles in 2025), you can contribute to a non-deductible Traditional IRA and then immediately convert it to a Roth.

3. Donor-Advised Funds (DAF)

For those with significant charitable goals, a DAF allows you to "bunch" several years of donations into a single year. You get an immediate tax deduction for the total amount today, but you can distribute the money to charities over the next decade.

Your New Financial Identity

As you finish this book, remember: Taxes are likely your single largest expense in life. By reducing that expense through smart planning, you aren't just "saving money"—you are buying back your time.

The refund check is a rearview mirror. The strategies in this book are your windshield. It's time to look forward.

CONCLUSION: THE POST-SEASON STRATEGY SESSION

You've made it through the "April 15th Pivot." You understand the psychology of the refund, the power of the W-4, and the importance of tax-efficient "buckets."

But reading is only the first step. Execution is where wealth is won. Now that the rush of tax season is over, it's the perfect time for a calm, strategic look at your 5-year wealth plan. We can help you:

1. Calculate your exact "Sweet Spot" for withholdings.
2. Audit your investment accounts for tax efficiency.
3. Determine if advanced tools like the Mega-Backdoor Roth are available to you.

| 21 |

MAY: THE ENTREPRENEUR'S SPRING CLEANING

The Great Separation

Drawing the Line Between You and Your Business

We've all been there: You're at the grocery store, you realize you're out of printer ink, and you grab a pack with your personal debit card. Or perhaps it's the other way around—you use the business credit card to pay for a quick lunch because it was the first one you pulled out of your wallet.

In the moment, it feels like a small convenience. In reality, you are creating a "financial fog" that obscures your profit and creates significant legal risk. To have a profitable year ahead, we must start with The Great Separation.

The "Piercing the Corporate Veil" Risk

Most entrepreneurs set up an LLC or a Corporation to protect their personal assets (like their home and personal savings) from business liabilities. This protection is often called the Corporate Veil.

However, if you treat your business bank account like a personal piggy bank, a court can rule that your business is not actually a separate entity. This is known as "piercing the corporate veil." If this happens, your personal assets are suddenly on the table to satisfy business debts or legal judgments.

The takeaway: Mixing funds isn't just a messy accounting habit; it's a hole in your legal armor.

The Clean Break: A Step-by-Step Guide

To "Spring Clean" your finances, you need a hard border between "Me, the Person" and "Me, the CEO." If you haven't done so already, follow this checklist immediately:

1. **Dedicated Business Checking**: This is your "Air Traffic Control." All revenue comes in here; all business bills go out from here.
2. **The Tax Savings Account**: A separate high-yield savings account where you move a percentage of every check (we'll discuss the "30% Rule" in Chapter 9).

3. **The Business Credit Card**: Use this strictly for recurring software subscriptions, inventory, and travel. It makes tracking expenses effortless and helps build your business credit score.

Pro-Tip: If you accidentally use the wrong card, don't panic. Record it immediately as an "Owner's Contribution" or "Owner's Draw" in your books to maintain the paper trail.

Audit Protection: Your First Line of Defense

Imagine the IRS sends you a letter requesting an audit. They ask to see the documentation for your business travel expenses.

- **Scenario A**: You hand over a bank statement filled with Starbucks runs, Netflix subscriptions, and Target trips, claiming that "some of those" were for the office.
- **Scenario B**: You hand over a clean, dedicated business statement where every single line item is a justifiable business expense.

Scenario B ends the audit quickly. By maintaining clear boundaries, you demonstrate "contemporaneous record-keeping"—the gold standard for tax compliance. It proves to the IRS (and yourself) that you are running a legitimate enterprise, not a hobby.

| 22 |

MODERN BOOKKEEPING—BEYOND THE SHOEBOX

Leveraging Technology to Gain Financial Clarity

For many entrepreneurs, "doing the books" involves a literal shoebox of receipts or a chaotic spreadsheet that only gets updated once a year. If you want to scale your business, you have to move beyond reactive accounting. Modern bookkeeping isn't about recording the past; it's about having the data to make decisions for the future.

The Cloud Revolution: Choosing Your Engine

The days of desktop-only software are over. Today, cloud-based accounting platforms allow you to access your financial health from your phone, your laptop, or even while sitting at a coffee shop.

- **QuickBooks Online (QBO)**: The industry standard. Most accountants prefer QBO because of its robust reporting and deep integration with other apps.
- **Xero**: Known for its user-friendly interface and "beautiful" design. It's a favorite for tech-savvy business owners and those with international needs.
- **FreshBooks**: Excellent for service-based entrepreneurs who prioritize invoicing and time-tracking over complex inventory management.

Automation is King: The "Categorize While You Sleep" Strategy

The secret to staying organized without losing your Sunday afternoons is the Bank Feed. By linking your dedicated business accounts (from Chapter 1) to your cloud software, every transaction is automatically pulled into your books.

You can set up Bank Rules to do the heavy lifting:

- **Rule**: Any transaction from "Adobe Systems" should be categorized as "Software/Subscription."
- **Rule**: Any deposit from "Stripe" should be categorized as "Sales Revenue."

With these rules in place, your software handles 80% of the work. Your job is simply to review and click "Match" once or twice a week.

The Monthly "Close": A CEO Power Move

The most dangerous way to run a business is by checking your bank balance to see if you can afford an expense. Your bank balance doesn't show you the taxes you owe or the bills that haven't cleared yet.

To graduate from "Owner" to "CEO," you must perform a Monthly Close. On the 1st of every month, reconcile your accounts and review your Profit & Loss (P&L) Statement.

The P&L tells you three vital things:

1. **Revenue Trends**: Are you making more or less than last month?
2. **Expense Creep**: Are those "small" monthly subscriptions eating your margins?
3. **Net Profit**: At the end of the day, after everyone else is paid, what is left for you?

| 23 |

THE ESTIMATED TAX MASTERY

Taking the Sting Out of Tax Season

There is a specific kind of "entrepreneurial anxiety" that sets in every April. It's that sinking feeling when your accountant reveals a tax bill that is five times larger than what you have in your savings account.

If you feel like you're constantly playing catch-up with the IRS, it's because you're treated differently than an employee. As the boss, no one is withholding taxes from your paycheck—you have to do it yourself. This chapter is about moving from "Surprise Bill" mode to "Complete Control" mode.

The "Surprise Bill" Prevention

The IRS operates on a "pay-as-you-go" system. They don't want to wait until April 15th to get their share of the income you earned last June. This is why small business owners are generally required to make Quarterly Estimated Tax Payments.

Mark these four dates in your calendar in red ink:

- April 15th (Q1)
- June 15th (Q2)
- September 15th (Q3)
- January 15th (Q4)

Missing these deadlines doesn't just result in a big bill later; it results in underpayment penalties and interest. By paying quarterly, you turn a giant, mountain-sized obstacle into four manageable molehills.

The 30% Rule: Your Financial Guardrail

The biggest mistake entrepreneurs make is treating 100% of their revenue as "spendable income." In reality, a chunk of every dollar you earn already belongs to the government.

The simplest way to manage this is the 30% Rule:

Every time you receive a payment from a client, immediately move 30% of that deposit into your dedicated "Tax Savings" account (which we set up in Chapter 21).

Why 30%? While your specific tax bracket may vary, this "rule of thumb" typically covers:

1. Federal Income Tax
2. Self-Employment Tax (Social Security and Medicare)
3. State Income Tax (in most states)

If you save 30% and your actual tax bill is only 22%, congratulations—you've just given yourself a "tax refund" bonus at the end of the year.

Safe Harbor Rules: Avoiding the Penalty Box

If your business is growing rapidly, it can be hard to predict exactly what you'll owe. This is where the Safe Harbor rules become your best friend.

Generally, the IRS won't charge you an underpayment penalty if you pay at least:

- 90% of the tax you owe for the current year, OR
- 100% of the tax shown on your return for the prior year (110% if your income is above a certain threshold).

By paying based on last year's numbers, you protect yourself from penalties even if your business has a massive, record-breaking year. It gives you the "Safe Harbor" to grow without fear of a surprise IRS "tax on your success."

| 24 |

EXPENSE TRACKING & THE TECH STACK

Lowering Your Bill with a Digital Fortress

The goal of Spring Cleaning isn't just to be tidy; it's to uncover value. In business, that value is found in deductions. Every dollar you spend on your business is a dollar you shouldn't have to pay taxes on—but only if you can prove it.

If you are still stuffing receipts into a glove box or trying to remember your business mileage at the end of the year, you are essentially leaving "tax-free money" on the table. This chapter introduces the tools that turn your smartphone into a tax-saving machine.

Receipt Management: Digitizing the Paper Trail

The IRS has officially entered the 21st century: they no longer require you to keep the original paper receipt as long as you have a legible, identical digital copy. Faded thermal paper is a liability; a cloud-stored PDF is an asset.

The Strategy: "Snap and Shred" Using tools like Dext (formerly Receipt Bank) or Hubdoc, you can take a photo of a receipt before you even leave the restaurant or the supply store.

- **How it works**: These apps use AI and OCR (Optical Character Recognition) to read the date, vendor, and amount.
- **The Benefit**: Once the photo is taken, the data is pushed directly into your accounting software (QuickBooks/Xero) and attached to the transaction.
- **The Result**: You can legally shred the paper. You've just audit-proofed that expense in under five seconds.

Mileage Tracking 2.0: Every Mile is Worth $0.70

For the 2025 tax year, the IRS standard mileage rate is $0.70 per mile. That may not sound like much, but a single 20-mile round trip to a client meeting is worth $14.00 in tax deductions. If you do that once a week, you're looking at over $700 in annual savings.

Stop using paper logs or "guesstimating" your odometer at the end of the year. Modern GPS-based apps like MileIQ run in the background of your phone:

1. It automatically detects when you're driving.
2. At the end of the day, you simply swipe right for business drives and swipe left for personal ones.
3. It generates a "contemporaneous log" that the IRS accepts without question.

Contractor Management: The W-9 Habit

Nothing ruins a relaxing January like chasing down a graphic designer or consultant you paid back in May because you need their tax ID for a 1099 form.

The Golden Rule of Contractors: > Never click "Send" on a payment until you have a signed W-9 Form in your hand (or your digital files).

Modern Onboarding: Use digital platforms like QuickBooks Contractor Portal, Gusto, or BILL to invite your contractors to fill out their tax info before work begins. This ensures:

- **Accuracy**: They type their own tax ID, reducing errors.
- **Compliance**: You are protected from "backup withholding" penalties (which can be as high as 24% of the payment).
- **Sanity**: When January rolls around, your 1099s are ready to file with a single click.

| 25 |

EVALUATING YOUR ENTITY STRUCTURE

When Your Business Outgrows Its Current Skin

As your business grows, the legal and tax structure you started with might become a burden rather than a benefit. If you are seeing consistent profits, you may be overpaying the IRS simply because of your "entity status." This chapter is about moving beyond the basics to ensure your business structure is optimized for your current revenue level.

Is It Time for an S-Corp?

Most small businesses start as a Sole Proprietorship or a Single-Member LLC. Under these structures, the IRS views you and your business as one and the same for tax purposes. You pay a 15.3% Self-Employment Tax on every single dollar of profit you earn.

An S-Corp (S-Corporation) is a tax election that allows you to split your income into two buckets:

1. **Reasonable Salary**: You pay yourself a W-2 wage. You pay the 15.3% tax only on this amount.
2. **Distributions**: The remaining profit is paid to you as a shareholder distribution. This bucket is exempt from the 15.3% self-employment tax.

The Math in Action: If your business profits $100,000 as a Sole Proprietor, you pay 15.3% on the full $100,000. As an S-Corp, if you pay yourself a $60,000 "reasonable salary," you only pay that 15.3% tax on the $60,000. You could potentially save over $6,000 a year just by changing your tax designation.

The LLC Myth: Legal vs. Tax Designation

One of the biggest points of confusion for entrepreneurs is the difference between an LLC and an S-Corp.

- **LLC (Limited Liability Company)**: This is a legal structure created at the state level. It protects your personal assets from business lawsuits (as discussed in Chapter 1).
- **S-Corp**: This is a tax designation at the federal level.

You don't have to "become a corporation" to get S-Corp benefits. You can keep your LLC for its simplicity and legal protection while asking the IRS to tax you as an S-Corp by filing Form 2553.

When to Pivot: Key Revenue Milestones

An S-Corp isn't free. It requires you to run formal payroll and file a separate business tax return (Form 1120-S). Because of these extra administrative costs—usually around $2,000 to $3,000 per year—the "switch" only makes sense once your savings outweigh the costs.

Profit Level	Recommendation
$0 – $40k	**Stay a Sole Prop/LLC.** The administrative costs of an S-Corp will likely eat up any tax savings.
$40k – $60k	**The "Grey Area."** Start talking to your accountant. If you expect growth next year, it may be time to prepare.
$60k – $80k+	**The Sweet Spot.** This is usually where the tax savings significantly outweigh the costs of payroll and accounting.

The "Reasonable Salary" Rule: The IRS requires that your S-Corp salary be "reasonable" for your industry. If you make $200,000 in profit but only pay yourself a $20,000 salary to avoid taxes, you are inviting an audit. A good rule of thumb is to pay yourself what it would cost to hire someone else to do your job.

Conclusion: Your Profitable Path Forward

From Financial Fog to CEO Clarity

Spring cleaning is more than a seasonal chore; it is a psychological reset. By following the steps in this book—separating your accounts, automating your bookkeeping, mastering your taxes, and optimizing your entity—you have done something most business owners never do: you have taken control.

The "Financial Fog" of past tax seasons doesn't have to be your permanent reality. When your books are clean, your deductions are tracked, and your structure is optimized, you stop making decisions based on "gut feelings" or your bank balance. You start making decisions based on data.

You are no longer just an employee of your own company; you are the CEO. And a CEO's most valuable asset isn't just money—it's the peace of mind that comes from knowing their foundation is solid.

JUNE: MAJOR LIFE CHANGES & YOUR TAXES

The Marriage & Divorce "Math"

For years, tax planning for couples was relatively static. But in 2025, the thresholds have jumped, and the "cliff" for high earners has moved. Understanding these numbers isn't just for your accountant; it's the key to keeping more of what you earn as your family structure changes.

The 2025 Filing Status Update

The most immediate change you'll notice is the significant increase in the Standard Deduction. For many families, itemizing (listing out individual deductions like mortgage interest) no longer makes sense because the "floor" is now so high.

Filing Status	2025 Standard Deduction
Single	$15,750
Married Filing Jointly	$31,500
Head of Household	$23,625

The Strategy: If you get married on December 31st, the IRS considers you married for the entire year. This means you instantly double your standard deduction to $31,500. For a couple where one person earns significantly more than the other, this "instant" deduction can result in a massive tax refund in your first year of marriage.

The "Marriage Penalty" vs. "Bonus"

Does getting married actually save you money? It depends on your "math."

- **The Marriage Bonus**: This usually happens when one spouse earns the majority of the household income. By filing jointly, the high-earner's income is pulled down into the lower tax brackets of the lower-earning spouse. In 2025, with the widened 12% and 22% brackets, this "bonus" is more accessible than ever.

- **The Marriage Penalty**: This typically hits "power couples"—two high earners with similar incomes. When you combine two large salaries, you might find yourselves pushed into the 32% or 35% brackets much faster than you would have as two single filers.

Pro Tip: In 2025, the 24% bracket for married couples now extends all the way to $394,600. If your combined income is under this mark, you likely still enjoy a "marriage neutral" or "bonus" scenario.

Divorce & Alimony: The Permanent Shift

If your life is moving in a different direction, the tax implications of divorce are equally stark. A common misconception persists that alimony is "tax-deductible."

Under the laws solidified for 2025:

1. **For Payers**: Alimony payments are not deductible. You pay the support with "after-tax" dollars.
2. **For Recipients**: Alimony is not taxable income. You receive the full amount without owing the IRS a dime.

The Negotiation Warning: This shift has fundamentally changed how settlements are negotiated. Because the payer no longer gets a tax break, they often have less "liquid" cash to offer. Conversely, the recipient needs to realize that $3,000 in tax-free alimony is worth much more than $3,000 in taxable wages.

| **27** |

EXPANDING THE FAMILY

New Credits for 2025

The days of a flat $1,000 or $2,000 credit are behind us. Whether you are welcoming a newborn or bringing a child home through adoption, the federal government has increased its "investment" in your family.

The Enhanced Child Tax Credit (CTC)

The Child Tax Credit has received a permanent boost for 2025. This isn't just a deduction; it's a dollar-for-dollar reduction of your tax bill.

- **The Amount**: The credit has jumped to $2,200 per qualifying child (up from $2,000).
- **Refundability Rules**: If your tax bill is already zero, you don't lose the credit. You can receive up to $1,700 per child as a refund (the "Additional Child Tax Credit").

- **Phase-Outs**: The full credit remains available for those earning up to $200,000 (Single) or $400,000 (Married Filing Jointly), making it accessible for almost all middle-class families.

Important Note: Starting in 2026, this $2,200 amount will be indexed for inflation, meaning your credit will likely grow as the cost of living rises.

"Trump Accounts" for Children (2025–2028)

Perhaps the most discussed update in 2025 is the introduction of Trump Accounts. These are tax-exempt savings accounts designed to give children a financial head start from birth.

- **The $1,000 Kickstart**: For any U.S. citizen child born between January 1, 2025, and December 31, 2028, the federal government provides a one-time $1,000 seed contribution.
- **Growth & Contributions**: Parents, grandparents, and even employers can contribute up to $5,000 annually. The funds are invested in broad U.S. equity index funds and grow tax-deferred.
- **The "IRA" Pivot**: Once the child turns 18, the account can be converted into a traditional IRA. If left untouched, that initial $1,000 and subsequent growth could potentially turn into a massive retirement nest egg by the time the child reaches age 65.

The Adoption Credit: A Historic Change

Adoption is a beautiful but expensive journey. In 2025, the tax code offers more relief than ever before by making a portion of the Adoption Credit refundable for the first time since 2011.

- **Maximum Credit**: You can claim up to $17,280 in qualified adoption expenses (legal fees, travel, court costs).
- **The Refundable Jump**: For the first time, up to $5,000 of this credit is refundable. This means even if you have zero tax liability for the year, you could still receive a $5,000 check from the IRS to help offset adoption costs.+1
- **Special Needs**: If you adopt a child with special needs, you may be eligible for the full credit amount, even if your actual out-of-pocket expenses were lower.

HOMEOWNERSHIP & THE $40,000 SALT JUMP

The Cap Has Been Raised.

For years, homeowners in high-tax states were frustrated by the $10,000 cap on State and Local Tax (SALT) deductions. In 2025, that ceiling has finally been lifted, though it comes with some "fine print" for high earners.

The New SALT Cap: Relief at Last

The SALT deduction allows you to deduct the property taxes you pay on your home, plus either your state income tax or sales tax.

- The Big Jump: For the 2025 tax year, the deduction cap has been raised from $10,000 to $40,000 ($20,000 if Married Filing Separately).

- The Income Phase-Out: This relief is designed for the middle and upper-middle class. If your Modified Adjusted Gross Income (MAGI) exceeds $500,000, the cap begins to shrink by 30 cents for every dollar over that limit. Once you hit $600,000 in income, you revert to the old $10,000 cap.
- Itemizing is Back: With a $40,000 limit, many families who previously took the standard deduction will find that itemizing on Schedule A now yields much higher savings.

Selling the "Starter Home"

If your big move involves selling your current home, the "2-out-of-5-years" rule remains your best friend.

- The Exclusion: You can still exclude up to $500,000 in capital gains from your income if you are married ($250,000 for singles).
- The Residency Rule: To qualify, you must have owned and lived in the house as your primary residence for at least two of the five years leading up to the sale.
- A 2025 Warning: While there has been talk in Congress about increasing these limits to account for home price inflation, they remain at $500k/$250k for now. If your home has appreciated significantly more than that, you may owe capital gains tax on the surplus.

New Vehicle Interest Deduction: A 2025 Surprise

If your move requires a new set of wheels to get the kids to school or yourself to a new office, the OBBBA added a brand-new "above-the-line" deduction that doesn't even require you to item-ize.

- The Deduction: You can deduct up to $10,000 in interest paid on a loan for a qualified passenger vehicle.
- The "Made in USA" Catch: The vehicle must be new (not used) and must have undergone its final assembly in the United States.
- Income Limits: This benefit phases out for single filers earning over $100,000 and married couples earning over $200,000.
- VIN Requirement: You must report the Vehicle Identification Number (VIN) on your tax return to prove the car was American-made.

| 29 |

THE CAREER PIVOT & RELOCATION

Personal Life and Professional Evolution

In this chapter, we navigate the fine line between personal life and professional evolution, and how the IRS views the expenses you incur while moving toward your next big break.

Job Hunting & Relocation: The Permanent Change

For decades, Americans could deduct the cost of moving for a new job. However, the One Big Beautiful Bill Act (OBBBA) signed in July 2025 has finalized a major shift in this area.

- **The Federal Reality**: For the 2025 tax year, federal moving expense deductions remain suspended for almost all private-sector employees.
- **The "Elite" Exceptions**: Only active-duty military members moving under permanent change of station (PCS) orders—and, as of 2025, certain members of the U.S.

Intelligence Community—can deduct these costs on a federal level.

- **The State Loophole**: While the federal government has tightened its belt, some states (like Massachusetts and California) may still allow moving deductions on your state return.

The Strategy: If your new employer offers a relocation "bonus," be aware that it is considered taxable income. Ask for a "gross-up," where the company covers the extra tax liability so your actual moving budget doesn't shrink.

The Remote Work Reality: Which State Gets Paid?

Moving to a new state while keeping your old job is the hallmark of the 2025 workforce. But your tax bill depends on a sneaky legal concept: the "Convenience of the Employer" rule.

If you live in Florida but work remotely for a firm in New York or Pennsylvania, you might face Double Taxation.

- **The Convenience Rule**: States like New York, Delaware, and Nebraska argue that if you could work in the office but choose to work from home for your own "convenience," they can tax 100% of your income—even if you never set foot in their state.
- **Reciprocity Agreements**: Before you move, check if your new state has a "handshake deal" with your old one. States like Illinois and Indiana often agree not to tax each other's residents, saving you from filing two separate state returns.

Side-Hustle Startup: Tracking from Day 1

2025 has seen a massive surge in "passion projects" becoming primary income sources. If you launched a business this year, the IRS allows you a "launch pad" deduction.

- **The $5,000 Rule**: You can deduct up to $5,000 in startup costs (market research, legal fees, website hosting) and $5,000 in organizational costs (LLC filing fees) in your first year.
- **The "Active" Requirement**: You can only claim these if your business actually starts operations. If you spend $3,000 on a logo but never sell a product, the IRS considers that a non-deductible personal hobby.
- **100% Bonus Depreciation**: A 2025 win from the OBBBA—the 100% bonus depreciation has been made permanent. This means if you buy a $2,000 laptop for your new business, you can write off the entire cost in Year 1 rather than spreading it out over five years.

| 30 |

RETIREMENT & THE NEW "SENIOR DEDUCTION"

Thinking About The Future

Retirement isn't just about spending down your nest egg; it's about managing how much of that egg the government takes. This year, the rules for both living seniors and those passing on an inheritance have shifted in favor of wealth preservation.

Age 65 Milestone: The $6,000 "Senior Bonus"

The most notable addition in 2025 is the Senior Bonus Deduction. Unlike the standard deduction, which increases for seniors, this is a brand-new, standalone deduction designed to shield more retirement income from tax.

1. **The Amount**: You can claim an additional $6,000 deduction if you are age 65 or older by December 31, 2025.
2. **Double for Couples**: If you and your spouse are both 65+, the bonus doubles to $12,000 on a joint return.

3. **The "Stacking" Effect**: This is in addition to your existing standard deduction. For a 65-year-old single filer in 2025, the total "tax-free" floor looks like this:

   - **Standard Deduction: $15,750**
   - **Existing Senior Addition: $2,000**
   - **New Senior Bonus: $6,000**
   - **Total Tax-Free Income: $23,750**

The Phase-Out: To ensure this helps those who need it most, the bonus begins to shrink once your Modified Adjusted Gross Income (MAGI) hits $75,000 (Single) or $150,000 (Joint). It disappears entirely at $175,000 and $250,000, respectively.
Inheritances: The "Step-Up" survives 2025

A major concern during the 2025 legislative sessions was whether the government would eliminate the "Step-Up in Basis." Fortunately for heirs, this vital rule remains intact under the OBBBA.

- **How it Works**: If you inherit your parents' home or a portfolio of stocks mid-year, the "cost basis" of those assets is reset to their fair market value on the day the original owner passed away.
- **The Mid-Year Strategy**: If you inherit a house in June that was bought for $50,000 in 1980 but is worth $600,000 today, you can sell it in July and owe zero capital gains tax on that $550,000 of growth.
- **2025 Reporting**: Be sure to get a formal appraisal as of the date of death. With home values fluctuating in 2025, having that "death day" value documented is the only way to prove your tax-free status to the IRS.

The New Estate Tax Ceiling

If you are worried about the "Death Tax," 2025 brought more good news. The federal estate tax exemption—the amount you can pass on without paying the 40% tax—has been permanently increased and indexed.

- **For 2025**: The individual exemption is $13.99 million.
- **Looking Toward 2026**: Under the OBBBA, this will jump to $15 million per person on January 1st.

Pro Tip: If you are nearing these limits, 2025 is the year to utilize "lifetime gifting" to lock in these historically high thresholds before any future political shifts.

CONCLUSION: YOUR "LIFE PIVOT" ROADMAP

Timing is everything. Because the IRS looks at your status on December 31st to determine your taxes for the whole year, the actions you take this quarter will define your next tax return.

The "Life Event" Checklist

If you've moved, married, or grown your family recently, check off these essential administrative steps:

- **Update the Social Security Administration (SSA)**: If you changed your name, file Form SS-5 immediately. The IRS computer systems will reject your return if the name on your 1040 doesn't match the SSA's records.

Notify the IRS of an Address Change: Don't just rely on the Post Office to forward your mail. File Form 8822 (Change of Address) to ensure you receive critical IRS correspondence and refund checks.

◦ **Submit a New Form W-4 to Your Employer**: You are required to give your employer a new W-4 within 10 days of a change in marital status. This prevents "sticker shock" next April by adjusting your withholding now.

◦ **Register New Dependents**: Ensure newborns or newly adopted children are registered with the SSA to receive their Social Security Number (SSN) or Adoption Taxpayer Identification Number (ATIN) before tax season.

◦ **Notify the Health Insurance Marketplace**: If you receive a premium tax credit, a change in family size or household income must be reported to the Marketplace immediately to avoid having to "pay back" credits at year-end.

Important 2025/2026 Deadlines

Mark these dates on your calendar to stay ahead of the "One Big Beautiful Bill" requirements:

Milestone	Deadline
Q3 Estimated Tax Payment	September 15, 2025
Final 2025 Life Status Date	December 31, 2025
Q4 Estimated Tax Payment	January 15, 2026
2025 Tax Filing Deadline	April 15, 2026

JULY: THE MID-YEAR TAX CHECK-UP

HE PAYCHECK "PAY RAISE" STRATEGY

How to Stop Giving Uncle Sam an Interest-Free Loan

The Hidden Mismatch of 2025

The Core Issue: Most Americans are currently overpaying the IRS every single month without realizing it.

- **The 2025 OBBBA Factor**: The Omnibus Budget and Balanced Budget Act (OBBBA) of 2025 introduced significant tax cuts and bracket adjustments. However, the IRS standard withholding tables—the "default" settings your employer uses—often lag behind these legislative changes.
- **The Result**: Your employer is likely withholding money based on outdated projections. You are paying "Old World" taxes in a "New World" tax environment.

- **The Opportunity**: Because we are at the halfway point, adjusting your withholding now allows you to "capture" the savings from the first six months and spread them across your remaining paychecks for the year.

The "Interest-Free Loan" Trap

The Psychological Shift: A large tax refund is not a "bonus" from the government; it is a sign of poor cash flow management.

- **The Opportunity Cost**: If you are on track for a $5,000 refund, that is roughly $415 per month that you didn't have access to.
- **Inflation vs. Savings**: While the government holds your money at 0% interest, you could have placed that $415/month into a High-Yield Savings Account (HYSA) or used it to pay down high-interest debt.
- **Wealth Building**: Active wealth builders prioritize liquidity. Every dollar held by the IRS is a dollar that isn't working for you. The goal of the Halftime Reset is to get that money back into your bank account starting with your next pay period.

Executing the W-4 Adjustment

The Action Plan: You don't need to be a CPA to fix your cash flow. You just need 15 minutes and the right data.

- **Step 1**: Gather Your Data. You will need your most recent pay stub (and your spouse's, if filing jointly) and a copy of your 2024 tax return.

- **Step 2**: Use the IRS Withholding Estimator. Navigate to the official IRS.gov estimator tool. It will ask for your year-to-date (YTD) federal tax withheld—this is the "Halftime Score" we need.
- **Step 3**: The "New" W-4. The estimator will tell you exactly how to fill out a new Form W-4.
    - **Tip**: If you've already overpaid in the first half of the year, you may be able to significantly reduce withholding for the second half, resulting in a massive "pay raise" for the rest of 2025.
- **Step 4**: Submit to HR. Most companies allow you to update this through an online payroll portal (like ADP or Workday) instantly.

The Halftime Win: By adjusting your W-4 in July, you effectively give yourself a monthly raise for the rest of the year, providing the capital you need to fund the strategies we will discuss in Chapters 33 and 34.

| 32 |

SAFE HARBOR—AVOIDING THE "PENALTY PUNCH"

Defending Your Wealth Against Underpayment Interest

The IRS "Pay-As-You-Go" Reality

The Misconception: Many taxpayers believe they can simply "settle up" on April 15th.

- **The Rule**: The U.S. tax system is "pay-as-you-go." If you don't pay enough throughout the year via withholding or estimated payments, the IRS charges an underpayment penalty—which is essentially interest on the money you should have sent them earlier.
- **Why it Matters Now**: With interest rates remaining a factor in 2025, these penalties are more expensive than they used to be. Avoiding them is an immediate "win" for your ROI.

- **The Goal**: To hit the "Safe Harbor" targets so you can keep your money in your accounts as long as possible without triggering IRS fines.

PLAIN-ENGLISH SAFE HARBOR RULES

The Strategy: You don't have to be 100% accurate to avoid penalties; you just have to meet one of these three benchmarks:

Rule	Who it's for	The Requirement
The 90% Rule	Most Taxpayers	Pay at least **90%** of your total 2025 tax liability by year-end.
The 100% Rule	Standard Income	Pay **100%** of the tax shown on your *previous* year's (2024) return.
The 110% Rule	High Earners	If your 2024 AGI was over $150k, you must pay **110%** of last year's tax to be "safe."

Pro Tip: For most clients, the 110% rule is the "gold standard." It's a fixed number based on last year's return, making it a predictable target regardless of how much you earn this year.

Windfall Management & The "Catch-Up"

The Mid-Year Audit: Did the first half of 2025 bring unexpected income?

- Trigger Events: Did you sell a business, a primary residence with a large gain, or a significant block of stock in Q1 or Q2?
- The "Lump Sum" Trap: If you had a massive windfall in May but wait until April 2026 to pay the tax, the IRS will backdate the penalty to the quarter the income was realized.
- The Solution: Use the "Halftime Reset" to calculate the tax owed on that specific windfall. Making a "catch-up" estimated payment now stops the penalty clock from ticking.

The September 15th Preview

The Deadline: Your next major milestone is the Q3 Estimated Tax deadline.

- Mark the Calendar: September 15, 2025.
- The "July Adjustment" Benefit: If you adjusted your W-4 (from Chapter 1) to account for your windfall, you might not even need to write a separate check for Q3.
- Action Item: Review your YTD "Total Tax Paid" (withholding + estimated payments) against your 110% Safe Harbor target today. If you're short, we have two months to fix it before the next deadline.

The Halftime Win: By locking in your Safe Harbor status now, you eliminate "tax anxiety" for the rest of the year. You can invest your remaining cash flow aggressively, knowing the IRS is already satisfied.

RETIREMENT SECOND WIND

Calculating the Sprint to Your 2025 Contribution Goals

The 2025 Targets

The Landscape: The IRS adjusted contribution limits for 2025 to account for inflation. If you are still contributing based on 2024 numbers, you are leaving tax-advantaged space on the table.

- **401(k) / 403(b) / Most 457s:** $23,500 (up from $23,000).
- **IRA (Roth or Traditional):** $7,000 (remains steady, but eligibility phases-out are higher).
- **The "Age 50+" Bonus:** If you turn 50 this year, you qualify for catch-up contributions ($7,500 for 401ks; $1,000 for IRAs).
- **The Goal:** Every dollar placed in a traditional 401(k) reduces your taxable income for 2025 by a dollar. It is the most effective "instant" tax cut available to the high earner.

The "Catch-Up" Math

The Strategy: If you realize at this "halftime" mark that you've only contributed $5,000 of your $23,500 limit, you have a gap of $18,500 to close.

- **The Calculation**: Take your remaining gap and divide it by the number of pay periods left in the year (typically 12 if paid bi-weekly starting in July).
- **Example**: $18,500 ÷ 12 = $1,541 per paycheck.

Why July? If you wait until October to realize you're behind, the "per-paycheck" amount might become too large for your monthly budget to handle. By starting the "Second Wind" now, you smooth out the cash flow impact.

Don't Leave "Free Money" on the Table

The Match Audit: Many employers offer a matching contribution, but it often requires you to be contributing throughout the entire year.

- **The Trap**: If you "max out" your 401(k) too early (e.g., by September), and your company doesn't have a "True-Up" provision, you might miss out on the employer match for October, November, and December.
- **The Check**: Look at your benefits summary. If your employer matches 5% of your pay per pay period, you must ensure you are contributing at least 5% in every remaining paycheck of 2025 to capture every cent of that "free money."

The HSA "Triple Threat"

The Power Move: If you have a High Deductible Health Plan (HDHP), the Health Savings Account is the most tax-efficient vehicle in existence.

- **Triple Tax-Advantaged**: 1. Contributions are tax-deductible (or pre-tax via payroll). 2. Growth is tax-deferred. 3. Withdrawals for medical expenses are tax-free.
- **2025 Limits**: $4,300 for individuals; $8,550 for families.
- **Action Item**: If you haven't funded this yet, July is the perfect time to set up a recurring transfer to ensure you hit the max by December 31st.

The Halftime Win: Increasing your contributions now not only builds your future nest egg but also lowers the "Total Tax Owed" we calculated in Chapter 32—potentially making your "Safe Harbor" target even easier to hit.

| 34 |

MID-YEAR INVESTMENT HARVESTING

Why the Best Tax Deals are Found in July, Not December

The "Summer Version" of Tax-Loss Harvesting

The Core Strategy: Selling underperforming investments at a loss specifically to offset capital gains you've already realized this year (or expect to realize).

- Why wait until December? Most investors wait until the last week of the year to harvest losses. By then, everyone else is doing the same thing, which can drive prices down further or lead to missed opportunities if the market rallies in Q4.
- **Capturing Volatility**: Market dips in Q1 and Q2 are "locked in" tax benefits waiting to be claimed. If you harvest a loss in July, you have that "tax asset" ready to use against any gains you take in the second half of the year.

- **The $3,000 Bonus**: If your losses exceed your gains, you can use up to $3,000 of that excess to offset your ordinary income (like your salary), which is typically taxed at a much higher rate.

Navigating the 60-Day "Wash-Sale" Minefield

The Rule: The IRS disallows a tax loss if you buy a "substantially identical" security within 30 days before or after the sale.

- **The 61-Day Window**: To successfully claim the loss, you must be "out" of that specific position for 30 days on either side of the trade date.
- **Common Trap**: Dividend Reinvestment. If you sell a stock for a loss but have "Automatic Dividend Reinvestment" turned on, and a dividend hits within 30 days, that tiny reinvestment could trigger a wash-sale and disqualify your entire loss.
- **The Solution**: Switch to "Cash Dividends" in July for any assets you might want to harvest.
- **The "Workaround"**: If you sell an S&P 500 ETF (like VOO) at a loss, you can immediately buy a "Total Stock Market" ETF (like VTI).

They are correlated, but not "substantially identical" in the eyes of the IRS.

Dividend Efficiency Check

The Goal: Not all dividends are created equal. We want to ensure your portfolio is throwing off "Qualified" dividends rather than "Ordinary" ones.

- **Qualified Dividends**: Taxed at the lower capital gains rates (0%, 15%, or 20%). To qualify, you must hold the stock for more than 60 days.
- **Ordinary Dividends**: Taxed at your top marginal rate (up to 37%).
- **Action Item**: Review your brokerage "Income" tab. If you see high amounts of "Ordinary Dividends" in a taxable account, July is the time to consider moving those assets into a tax-deferred retirement account (from Chapter 3).

Rebalancing Without the Tax Hit

The Power Move: Using your harvested losses to rebalance your portfolio for free.

- **The Scenario**: Your Tech stocks have skyrocketed (overweight) and your International stocks have dipped (underweight).
- **The Execution**: 1. Sell the International "losers" to harvest the loss. 2. Sell just enough of the Tech "winners" to rebalance. 3. Use the loss from Step 1 to wipe out the tax from Step 2.
- **The Result**: You have a perfectly balanced portfolio for the second half of the year, and your tax bill remains $0.

The Halftime Win: Proactive harvesting in July gives you a "Tax Bank Account" that you can spend on gains throughout the rest of the year. It turns a market dip into a permanent tax reduction.

THE PAPERWORK AUDIT

Digitizing Your Deductions While the Memory is Fresh

The Six-Month Cleanse

The Reality Check: Paper receipts fade, and memories fade even faster. If you wait until next April to categorize a $400 dinner from last February, you likely won't remember if it was a business strategy session or a family birthday.

- **The IRS Standard**: To deduct an expense, you must prove the Amount, Date, Place, and Business Purpose.
- **The "Shoebox" Trap**: Physical receipts are a liability. They get lost, they're hard to search, and the thermal ink often disappears before you even file your return.
- **The July Solution**: Spend 30 minutes this month "cleansing" your first half of the year. Move every physical receipt into a cloud-based folder (Google Drive, Dropbox, or apps like Expensify).

- **The $75 Rule**: While the IRS generally doesn't require receipts for expenses under $75 (except for lodging), having a digital record protects you in an audit.

The Mileage Log "True-Up"

The Opportunity: For 2025, the IRS increased the business standard mileage rate to 70 cents per mile. This is one of the easiest deductions to lose if you aren't tracking it in real-time.

- **The 2025 Rates**: * Business: $0.70 / mile
- **Medical / Moving (Military)**: $0.21 / mile
  - **Charitable**: $0.14 / mile
- **The "Halftime" Check**: Compare your odometer or digital log (like MileIQ or QuickBooks Self-Employed) against your calendar.
- **Bridging the Gap**: If you realized you forgot to log trips in Q1, use your digital calendar now to reconstruct those trips while the meetings are still fresh in your mind.

HSA Triple-Tax Review

The Power Move: We mentioned the HSA in Chapter 3, but the "Audit" phase is about the Receipts.

- **The "Shoebox" for Healthcare**: The best way to use an HSA is to pay for medical expenses out of pocket today, let the HSA money grow tax-free in the market, and reimburse yourself years later.
- **The Catch**: To do this, you must keep every medical receipt (doctor co-pays, dental work, even sunscreen) for years.

- **Action Item**: Create a specific digital folder titled "Unreimbursed HSA Expenses." Every time you pay for a medical item out of pocket, scan the receipt there. This folder represents a "tax-free ATM" you can tap into anytime in the future.

The Digital Cloud Setup

The Infrastructure: Your goal is to be "Audit-Ready" by August 1st.

- **Categorization**: Organize your cloud storage by year and then by category (e.g., 2025 > Marketing, 2025 > Travel, 2025 > Healthcare).
- The "Audit-Proof" Standard:

  1. **Legible**: Can an IRS agent read the vendor name and date?
  2. **Complete**: Does it show the method of payment?
  3. **Backed Up**: Is it in the cloud and not just on a single phone or laptop?

The Halftime Win: By spending one hour now to organize the first 180 days of the year, you reduce your tax-prep time by 80% next spring. You aren't just saving paper; you're saving your future sanity.

CONCLUSION: THE "HALFTIME REPORT" STRATEGY

From Passive Taxpayer to Active Wealth Builder

The Halftime Scorecard

The Summary: You've now seen how the "Six-Month Rule" can change your entire 2025 financial outcome.

- **Chapter 31 &3 2 (Defense)**: You've learned how to fix the OBBBA withholding mismatch and lock in your Safe Harbor status to avoid penalties.
- **Chapter 33 & 34 (Offense)**: You've identified how to "sprint" your retirement contributions and harvest market volatility to create a "tax bank account" for future gains.
- **Chapter 35 (Infrastructure)**: You've set up the digital cloud system that makes April 15th a simple "click of a button" rather than a weekend of stress.

The "Halftime Report" Offer

Immediate Value: Most tax planning is retroactive (looking at what happened). Our approach is proactive (looking at what will happen).

- **The Offer**: Send us your most recent pay stub and your 2024 tax return.
- **The Deliverable**: We will run a 15-minute "Cash Flow Analysis" specifically tailored to the 2025 OBBBA tax cuts.

- **The Goal**: We want to see if you are one of the millions of Americans currently over-withholding. If you are, we'll show you exactly how to unlock that monthly cash flow immediately.

Your Q3 Planning Session

For High-Net-Worth Clients: If your situation involves business ownership, significant stock options (RSUs/ISO), or complex estate considerations, a 15-minute check-in isn't enough.

- **Strategic Planning**: July and August are the "quiet before the storm." Booking your Q3 Planning Session now ensures we can implement complex strategies (like Roth conversions or charitable "bunching") before the year-end deadlines.
- **The "Wait-List" Warning**: As we move into Q4, schedules fill up and the IRS deadlines for certain elections pass.

| **36** |

AUGUST: EDUCATION, KIDS, AND THE IRS

THE "HIRING YOUR KIDS" STRATEGY ($15,750 TAX-FREE)

For many business owners, one of the most powerful tax-planning tools is sitting right across the dinner table. With the passage of the One Big Beautiful Bill Act (OBBBA) in 2025, the incentives for involving your children in the family business have reached a historic high.

This strategy isn't just about teaching work ethic; it's a sophisticated method for shifting income from your high tax bracket into your child's 0% bracket.

The $15,750 Threshold: The Magic of the Standard Deduction

In 2025, the federal standard deduction for a single filer has increased to $15,750. This number is the "holy grail" for family tax planning.

When you hire your child, the first $15,750 you pay them in earned income is essentially "invisible" to the IRS. Because of the standard deduction, your child can earn up to this amount without paying a single cent in federal income tax. For a business owner in the 37% tax bracket, paying a child $15,750 can result in an immediate family tax savings of over $5,800.

Business Owners Only: Turning Chores into "Legitimate Work"

This strategy is a specialized "perk" for business owners. To make the deduction stick, you cannot simply give your child an allowance; you must pay them for legitimate work that is "ordinary and necessary" for your business.

The IRS has become increasingly comfortable with children performing modern business tasks. Examples of defensible, age-appropriate work include:

- Social Media Management: Capturing behind-the-scenes footage or scheduling posts.
- Administrative Tasks: Filing, shredding, data entry, or cleaning the office.
- Modeling/Marketing: Using their image in brochures or on your business website.
- Maintenance: Cleaning equipment or washing company vehicles.

Pro-Tip: To "audit-proof" this strategy, treat your child like any other employee. Create a formal job description, keep a digital log of their hours, and pay them a "reasonable wage" (what you would pay a stranger to do the same task). Always pay them via check or direct deposit from the business account to their own bank account to create a clear paper trail.

The Payroll Perk: The FICA Double-Win

While the income tax savings are great, the real "hidden gem" of the 2025 rules is the FICA exemption.

If your business is structured as a Sole Proprietorship, a Single-Member LLC, or a Partnership where both partners are the child's parents, you do not have to pay Social Security or Medicare (FICA) taxes on wages paid to your children under age 18. Furthermore, you are exempt from Federal Unemployment (FUTA) taxes until they turn 21.

Tax Type	Child < 18	Child 18–20	Child 21+
Federal Income Tax	0% (up to $15,750)	0% (up to $15,750)	0% (up to $15,750)
FICA (Social Security/Med)	Exempt	Subject to Tax	Subject to Tax
FUTA (Unemployment)	Exempt	Exempt	Subject to Tax

Note: This specific FICA/FUTA exemption does not apply if your business is an S-Corp or a C-Corp, though the income tax shifting benefits still remain.

By leveraging this strategy in 2025, you aren't just paying for help—you're effectively funding your child's future, their 529 plan, or even their first Roth IRA with "pre-tax" dollars that the IRS never touches.

THE 2025 529 REVOLUTION

The College Bucket

For years, 529 plans were seen as "college-only" buckets. If you didn't have a child in a four-year university, the money felt locked away.

But 2025 has brought a tidal wave of changes. Thanks to the One Big Beautiful Bill Act (OBBBA), the 529 is no longer just a college fund—it's a comprehensive family education and wealth-building tool.

Doubling Down on K–12: From $10k to $20k

The most immediate shift for parents of younger children is the massive increase in K–12 flexibility. Previously, you could only withdraw $10,000 per year for private school tuition.

- **The 2025 Upgrade**: While the limit remains $10,000 for the remainder of 2025, the OBBBA has officially set the stage for a $20,000 annual withdrawal cap per student starting January 1, 2026.

- **The Strategy**: If you have been hesitant to use 529 funds for private elementary or high school because the "cap was too low," you can now plan for a much more aggressive withdrawal strategy to cover nearly double the tuition costs tax-free.

New Qualified Expenses: Tutoring, Testing, and Homeschooling

Starting in July 2025, the definition of what counts as a "qualified expense" exploded. You are no longer restricted to just "tuition." You can now use 529 funds for:

- **Professional Tutoring**: Fees paid to licensed or expert instructors (unrelated to the student) for academic support.
- **Standardized Testing**: SAT, ACT, AP exam fees, and even the prep courses required to ace them.
- **Homeschooling Resources**: For the first time, "structured homeschool curricula" and instructional materials are federally recognized as qualified expenses.
- **Specialized Therapy**: Educational therapies for students with diagnosed learning differences (like ADHD or dyslexia) provided by accredited practitioners.

The Roth IRA Escape Hatch: A $35,000 Safety Net

The #1 fear parents had about 529s was "overfunding." What if the child gets a full scholarship? What if they don't go to college?

The 2025 rules provide a permanent "escape hatch" through the 529-to-Roth IRA rollover. You can now roll over up to a lifetime maximum of $35,000 from a 529 plan into a Roth IRA for the beneficiary.

The "Fine Print" Requirements:

1. **The 15-Year Rule**: The 529 account must have been open for at least 15 years.
2. **The 5-Year Rule**: You cannot roll over any contributions (or their earnings) made within the last five years.
3. **Annual Limits**: The rollover is subject to annual Roth IRA contribution limits ($7,000 in 2025). This means moving the full $35,000 will typically take about 5 years of transfers.
4. **Earned Income**: The child must have earned income at least equal to the amount being rolled over (which ties back perfectly to the "Hiring Your Kids" strategy in Chapter 1!).

Summary Table: 529 Rules at a Glance (2025)

Category	Old Rule	New 2025/2026 Rule
K-12 Tuition Cap	$10,000 / year	$20,000 / year (starting 2026)
Tutoring & Test Fees	Non-Qualified	Qualified (Tax-Free)
Homeschool Materials	Non-Qualified	Qualified (Tax-Free)
Unused Funds	10% Penalty + Tax	Roth IRA Rollover (Up to $35k)

| 38 |

COLLEGE CREDITS—AOTC VS. LLC

The Great 1098 T & E

While 529 plans help you save for the future, education tax credits provide immediate relief on your tax return for expenses you are paying right now. In 2025, the IRS offers two primary "discounts" on your tax bill: the American Opportunity Tax Credit (AOTC) and the Lifetime Learning Credit (LLC). Understanding the difference between them is the key to ensuring you don't leave thousands of dollars on the table.

American Opportunity Tax Credit (AOTC): The Undergraduate Powerhouse

The AOTC is generally the most valuable credit for students in their first four years of post-secondary education.

- **The Value:** You can claim up to $2,500 per eligible student, per year.

- **The Math**: The credit is calculated as 100% of the first $2,000 of qualified expenses, plus 25% of the next $2,000.
- **The Refundable Perk**: Most tax credits only reduce the tax you owe. However, the AOTC is 40% refundable. This means that if the credit brings your tax bill to zero, you can actually receive up to $1,000 as a refund check from the IRS.
- **Qualifications**: The student must be enrolled at least half-time in a program leading to a degree or recognized credential and must not have finished their first four years of higher education.

Lifetime Learning Credit (LLC): The Lifelong Learner's Safety Net

If your student has already graduated, is in grad school, or is simply taking a few classes to level up their career, the LLC is your go-to tool.

- **The Value**: You can claim up to $2,000 per tax return (calculated as 20% of the first $10,000 in expenses).
- **No "Four-Year" Limit**: Unlike the AOTC, which cuts off after four years, you can claim the LLC for an unlimited number of years.
- **Flexibility**: There is no "half-time" enrollment requirement. A student can take a single course at an eligible institution to improve job skills and still qualify.
- **The Catch**: The LLC is non-refundable. It can reduce your tax bill to zero, but it won't result in a refund check if you don't owe any taxes.

AOTC vs. LLC: A Quick Comparison

Feature	American Opportunity (AOTC)	Lifetime Learning (LLC)
Max Credit	Up to $2,500 per student	Up to $2,000 per return
Refundable?	Yes (Up to $1,000)	No
Years Available	First 4 years only	Unlimited years
Degree Required?	Yes	No
Enrollment	At least half-time	One course or more

Income Limits: Don't Get Phased Out

Both credits are designed for middle-income families, and the IRS "phases out" the benefits as your income rises. For 2025, the income thresholds for both credits are identical:

- **Married Filing Jointly**: The credit begins to decrease once your Modified Adjusted Gross Income (MAGI) hits $160,000 and disappears entirely at $180,000.
- **Single/Head of Household**: The phase-out range is $80,000 to $90,000.

Strategic Note: You cannot "double-dip." You can't claim both the AOTC and the LLC for the same student in the same year. However, if you have two children in college, you could potentially claim the AOTC for your freshman and the LLC for your grad student on the same tax return.

THE 2025 BABY BONUS & FUTURE SAVINGS

What is a Trump Account?

While earlier chapters focused on active students, the One Big Beautiful Bill Act (OBBBA) of 2025 introduced groundbreaking measures for the youngest members of your family. Whether you are welcoming a newborn or managing the costs of a growing household, the 2025 rules provide a significant financial "seed" to help bridge the gap between today's expenses and tomorrow's wealth.

The Federal Seed Account: A $1,000 Head Start

One of the most talked-about features of the new law is the creation of Trump Accounts (officially categorized under Section 530A). For children born between January 1, 2025, and December 31, 2028, the federal government has launched a pilot program to encourage early investing.

- **The Grant**: Eligible newborns can receive a one-time $1,000 federal contribution to seed their account.
- **How it Works**: Parents must "elect" to open the account using the child's Social Security number (often through a simple digital application at trumpaccounts.gov).
- **The Growth Power**: These accounts are designed for long-term compounding. Funds are typically invested in broad-based American stock indices and cannot be touched until the child turns 18. At that point, the account can be rolled over into a Traditional IRA, creating a seamless path to retirement savings before the child even holds their first full-time job.

Enhanced Child Tax Credit: $2,200 per Child

The Child Tax Credit (CTC) has long been a staple for family tax planning, but 2025 brings a permanent boost to its value.

- **The New Max**: The credit has increased from $2,000 to $2,200 per qualifying child under age 17.
- **Refundability**: If your tax bill is already zero, you don't lose the credit. You can receive up to $1,700 per child as a refund (the "Additional Child Tax Credit").
- **Inflation Protection**: For the first time, this $2,200 base amount is now indexed to inflation starting in 2026, meaning the credit will finally keep pace with the rising cost of living.
- **The Phase-Out**: The full credit is available for married couples earning up to $400,000 ($200,000 for single parents), making it a benefit that reaches nearly every middle-class family in the country.

Student Loan Interest: An "Above-the-Line" Win

For parents still paying off their own degrees or recent grads starting their careers, the IRS continues to offer a "hidden" deduction that doesn't require you to itemize.

- **The Deduction**: You can deduct up to $2,500 of interest paid on qualified student loans.
- **No Itemizing Required**: This is an "above-the-line" deduction, meaning it reduces your Adjusted Gross Income (AGI) directly. You get this benefit even if you take the standard deduction.
- **2025 Income Limits**: To claim the full deduction, your Modified AGI must be below $170,000 (married) or $85,000 (single). The benefit phases out completely at $200,000 and $100,000, respectively.

Key Takeaway: By combining the $2,200 Child Tax Credit with the $1,000 Federal Seed Account, a child born in 2025 effectively enters the world with a $3,200 tax-advantaged head start.

| **40** |

AUGUST SALES TAX HOLIDAYS

Save While You Shop

As summer winds down, the "August Opportunity" begins. In 2025, over a dozen states are participating in sales tax holidays designed to ease the burden of back-to-school shopping. For parents, it's a way to save up to 10% instantly on essential gear; for business owners, it's a strategic window to boost revenue and clear inventory before the fall.

State-by-State Savings: Where to Shop Tax-Free

While every state has slightly different rules and "price caps" (the maximum price an item can be to qualify), the general categories remain consistent: clothing, school supplies, and technology.

State	2025 Dates	Key Exemptions & Price Caps
Florida	Aug 1–31	Computers ($1,500), Clothing ($100), School Supplies ($50)
Ohio	Aug 1–14	The "Everything" Holiday: Almost all items $500 or less
Texas	Aug 8–10	Clothing, Backpacks, and School Supplies (all under $100)
Missouri	Aug 1–3	Computers ($1,500), Software ($350), Clothing ($100)
Tennessee	July 25–27	Computers ($1,500), Clothing ($100), School Supplies ($100)
Virginia	Aug 1–3	Clothing ($100), School Supplies ($20), Energy Star ($2,500)

Note: Some states, like Massachusetts (Aug 9–10), offer a "blanket" holiday on almost all retail items up to $2,500.

The "Small Business" Twist: Leveraging the Holiday

If you are a business owner, these holidays aren't just for your personal shopping; they are a marketing goldmine. Even if your business doesn't sell "traditional" school supplies, you can use the tax-free atmosphere to drive engagement:

1. Price-Adjust to the Cap: If you sell a product for $110 in a state with a $100 cap, consider a temporary $11 discount. By bringing the price under the cap, your customer saves

the discount plus the sales tax, making the deal feel twice as sweet.

2. The "Tax on Us" Promotion: If your state doesn't have a holiday—or your items don't qualify—run a "We Pay Your Sales Tax" weekend. It simplifies the math for the customer and creates the same psychological "win."

3. Inventory Clearance: Use the increased foot traffic (both digital and physical) during these weekends to bundle slow-moving items with tax-free essentials.

CONCLUSION & CALL TO ACTION (CTA)

The 2025 tax landscape has shifted the "cost of raising a family" into a "strategy for building family wealth." From the moment a child is born and receives their first $1,000 Federal Seed, to the teenage years spent earning a tax-free $15,750 in the family business, the OBBBA has provided the tools. Your job is simply to pick them up.

How We Can Help You Right Now:

- The "College Funding Review": Have a child entering high school or college? Let's run the numbers to ensure you're using 529s, AOTC credits, and the new $20k K–12 withdrawal limits in the most tax-efficient way possible.

- The Kid-Payroll Setup: Ready to move $15,750 out of your high tax bracket and into your child's 0% bracket? We can handle the W-2 setup, employment documentation, and "reasonableness" checks to ensure your strategy is audit-proof.

Stop leaving your family's "tax refund" on the table. Schedule your Family Tax Strategy Session today.

| **41** |

SEPTEMBER: THE RETIREMENT ROADMAP

THE SEPTEMBER 15TH DEADLINE

THE SAFETY NET

For many, September marks the end of summer and the return to routine. But in the world of tax strategy, September 15th is one of the most significant dates on the calendar. It represents a "safety net" moment—your last major opportunity to course-correct before the year's final quarter begins.

Missing this date doesn't just result in paperwork; it can lead to "The Penalty Punch," a series of avoidable IRS charges that eat away at your hard-earned capital.

Estimated Payment #3: Avoiding "The Penalty Punch"

If you are a freelancer, business owner, or investor, you likely don't have a HR department withholding taxes from a paycheck for you.

This means the IRS expects you to pay as you go.

The September 15th deadline is the due date for your third quarterly estimated tax payment. Many people mistakenly believe they can simply "settle up" in April. Unfortunately, the IRS views tax as a pay-as-you-earn system. If you wait until next spring to pay for the income you earned this summer, you could be hit with an underpayment penalty that is currently hovering around 7% to 8%, compounded daily.

Key Takeaway: If you haven't made a payment yet for your June, July, and August income, September 15th is your deadline to get square with Uncle Sam.

The Catch-Up Calculation: Mastering "Safe Harbor"

What happens if your business had a "blowout" summer? If your income spiked unexpectedly in Q3, your standard quarterly payment might not be enough to protect you from penalties.

To keep the IRS at bay, you need to understand the Safe Harbor rules. Generally, you can avoid underpayment penalties if you pay at least:

- 90% of the tax you owe for the current year, OR

- 100% of the tax shown on your prior year's return (this jumps to 110% if your Adjusted Gross Income was over $150,000).

By running a "Catch-Up Calculation" now, you can adjust your September payment to meet these Safe Harbor thresholds. This allows you to keep the rest of your cash working for you in your business or investments until April, rather than overpaying the government early.

S-Corp & Partnership Extensions: The Final Warning

If you operate your business as an S-Corporation or a Partnership and you filed for an extension back in March, the clock has officially run out.

September 15th is the absolute final deadline for these entities to file their tax returns. Unlike individual extensions (which run until October), business entity extensions expire now.

- **The Cost of Delay**: The penalty for late-filing a Partnership or S-Corp return is roughly $255 per month, per partner or shareholder.
- **The Ripple Effect**: If your business return is late, your personal K-1 is late, which complicates your personal filing in October.

This is the "Safety Net" chapter for a reason: by checking these three boxes now, you prevent the momentum of your Q4 from being stalled by unnecessary penalties and IRS notices.

| **42** |

THE 401(K) AND IRA
MAX-OUT PLAN

Retirement Strategy

If Chapter 1 was about building your "Safety Net," Chapter 2 is about accelerating your wealth. In the financial calendar, September isn't just a time for deadlines; it's a time for celebration.

National 401(k) Day: Your Wealth-Building Holiday

Celebrated on the Friday following Labor Day, National 401(k) Day is more than just a quirky calendar date. It serves as a strategic "half-time" marker. With roughly four months left in the year, this is the perfect moment to look at your year-to-date contributions and ask: "Am I on track to squeeze every possible tax advantage out of my income?"

The 401(k) remains the most powerful tool in your arsenal because it provides an immediate tax deduction while allowing your investments to grow tax-deferred for decades.

The 2025 Contribution Targets: New Limits, New Opportunities

For 2025, the IRS has once again adjusted contribution limits to account for inflation. If you haven't updated your automated deferrals since last year, you are likely underfunding your future self.

The 2025 Standard Targets:

- **401(k) / 403(b) Limit:** $23,500 (Up from $23,000 in 2024).
- **IRA / Roth IRA Limit**: $7,000 (Remaining steady from 2024).

The "Catch-Up" Power Moves:

If you are age 50 or older, you have the right to contribute even more. But 2025 introduces a unique "Super Catch-Up" window thanks to the SECURE 2.0 Act:

- **Age 50–59 and 64+:** You can contribute an additional $7,500, bringing your total 401(k) limit to $31,000.
- **The "Super Catch-Up" (Ages 60–63):** For a narrow window of individuals aged 60 to 63, the catch-up limit increases to $11,250, allowing for a massive total contribution of $34,750.

Account Type	Under Age 50	Age 50–59 / 64+	Age 60–63 (New!)

401(k) / 403(b)	$23,500	$31,000	$34,750
IRA (Traditional/ Roth)	$7,000	$8,000	$8,000

The Employer Match Audit: Don't Leave Free Money Behind

The most common mistake high-earning professionals make is "front-loading" their 401(k) so heavily in the first half of the year that they hit the $23,500 limit by August.

The Trap: Many employers only provide their matching contribution on a per-pay-period basis. If you stop contributing in September because you've already hit the limit, your employer may stop matching for the rest of the year.

How to perform a "Match Audit" this month:

1. **Check your pay stubs**: Look at the "Employer Match" line item.
2. **Review your Plan Document**: See if your company has a "True-Up" provision. If they don't, you must ensure you have enough "room" left in your limit to contribute at least a small percentage through your final December paycheck.
3. **Adjust your percentage**: If you are on track to max out too early, talk to HR about lowering your contribution percentage slightly so it stretches across every remaining pay period of the year.

By maximizing your own contributions and auditing your employer's match, you ensure that every dollar of "free money" is claimed before the clock strikes midnight on December 31st.

| 43 |

THE BACKDOOR ROTH SPOTLIGHT

A New Roth Strategy

For many high-achieving professionals, there is a frustrating ceiling in the tax code: once your income passes a certain level, you are told you "make too much" to contribute to a Roth IRA. In 2025, those phase-outs begin at $150,000 for single filers and $236,000 for those married filing jointly.

However, there is a legal, widely used strategy to bypass these limits. It's called the Backdoor Roth IRA, and September is the ideal time to execute it.

The High-Income Strategy: Sidestepping the Limits

The Backdoor Roth isn't a specific type of account; it's a two-step maneuver.

1. **Step One**: You make a "non-deductible" contribution to a Traditional IRA. Unlike a standard contribution, you don't get a tax break today, but there are no income limits on who can contribute.
2. **Step Two**: You immediately convert those funds into a Roth IRA.

Because you didn't take a tax deduction on the first step, the conversion is generally tax-free. Once the money is inside the Roth, it grows entirely tax-free for the rest of your life, and qualified withdrawals in retirement are also tax-free.

The Pro-Rata Rule: The "Tax Trap" to Avoid

While the strategy is legal, the IRS has a specific rule that can catch people off guard: the Pro-Rata Rule.

The IRS does not look at your IRAs as separate accounts. Instead, they lump all your Traditional, SEP, and SIMPLE IRAs together. If you have $93,000 in an old "Rollover IRA" from a previous job and you try to do a $7,000 Backdoor Roth, the IRS views your total IRA balance as $100,000.

In this scenario, only 7% of your conversion would be tax-free. The other 93% would be taxed as ordinary income.

The Fix: Before performing a Backdoor Roth, we often recommend "rolling over" any existing pre-tax IRA balances into your current employer's 401(k). This clears the path, making your Backdoor Roth conversion "clean" and tax-free.

The 2025 Window: Why Now?

September is the "sweet spot" for this strategy for three reasons:

1. **Paperwork Processing**: Conversions require clean documentation. Doing this in Q3 ensures your brokerage has ample time to issue the correct forms before the year-end rush.
2. **Market Growth**: The longer the money sits in a Traditional IRA before conversion, the more likely it is to gain value. You have to pay taxes on any gains during the conversion. Converting in September captures future Q4 growth inside the tax-free Roth wrapper instead.
3. **Legislative Uncertainty**: Tax laws are always subject to change. Executing your strategy now ensures you are "locked in" under the current 2025 rules, rather than scrambling in late December when new legislation might be on the table for 2026.

2025 Roth Strategy	Limit (Under 50)	Limit (50+)
Traditional IRA Contribution	$7,000	$8,000
Backdoor Conversion	No Limit	No Limit

| **44** |

INSURANCE AWARENESS

The Tax-Shield Connection

September is officially National Insurance Awareness Month. While most people view insurance as a "just in case" expense, savvy investors view it as a sophisticated tax shield.

In this chapter, we pivot from retirement accounts to the two most powerful ways to use insurance to protect your wealth from Uncle Sam: the Health Savings Account (HSA) and Permanent Life Insurance.

Health Insurance & The HSA: The Triple Tax Advantage

As we move through September, "Open Enrollment" for the following year is just around the corner. This is your window to select a plan that grants you access to the Health Savings Account (HSA)—arguably the most tax-efficient vehicle in the entire Internal Revenue Code.

The HSA is the only account that offers a Triple Tax Advantage:

1. **Tax-Free In**: Your contributions are 100% tax-deductible (or pre-tax via payroll).
2. **Tax-Free Growth**: Your balance can be invested in the stock market, and you pay $0 in capital gains or dividend taxes.
3. **Tax-Free Out**: Withdrawals are completely tax-free when used for qualified medical expenses.

Preparing for 2026: The IRS has already released the increased limits for next year. When you sit down for open enrollment this fall, keep these targets in mind:

- **Individual Coverage**: $4,400 (Up from $4,300 in 2025)
- **Family Coverage**: $8,750 (Up from $8,550 in 2025)
- **Catch-Up (Age 55+)**: An additional $1,000.

The Q3 Pro-Tip: Unlike a Flexible Spending Account (FSA), an HSA has no "use-it-or-lose-it" rule. If you are healthy and don't need the funds this year, you can let that money compound for decades, effectively turning it into a secondary retirement account for your healthcare needs in old age.

Life Insurance as a Tax Haven

While term insurance is great for basic protection, Permanent Life Insurance (such as Whole Life or Universal Life) serves as a high-level tax haven for those who have already maxed out their 401(k)s and IRAs.

1. Tax-Deferred Growth

The "Cash Value" inside a permanent policy grows tax-deferred, much like a retirement account. However, unlike a 401(k), there are no IRS limits on how much you can contribute (as long as the policy is structured correctly).

2. Tax-Free "Loans" (The Private Bank Strategy)

One of the most powerful "Power Moves" is the ability to access your cash value via policy loans. Because the IRS does not view a loan as "income," you can essentially spend your gains without triggering a tax bill. Many high-net-worth individuals use these tax-free loans to fund major purchases or business opportunities, all while the death benefit remains intact.

3. The Income-Tax-Free Inheritance

Finally, the most significant shield is the death benefit itself. While your heirs might be "walloped" by taxes when inheriting your 401(k) or IRA (often forced to withdraw and pay taxes within 10 years), a life insurance payout is generally 100% income-tax-free to your beneficiaries.

Why September Matters: Applying for or adjusting these policies takes time. If you wait until December, you may miss the window for medical underwriting or final signatures. Starting the conversation in September ensures your "tax shield" is fully operational before the new year begins.

PREPPING FOR THE HOLIDAY SPENDING HANGOVER

The Big Push

The final quarter of the year is notoriously the most expensive. Between personal gift-giving and business year-end pushes, cash flow can tighten quickly. Chapter 5 is about playing offense—ensuring you have the liquidity to enjoy the season while maximizing your final tax-saving opportunities.

The Holiday Budget: Protecting Your Tax Reserve

It's easy to get swept up in the spirit of the season and dip into funds that should be set aside for your April tax bill or your Q4 estimated payment (due January 15th).

The Q3 Strategy: * The "Tax First" Rule: Before committing to holiday bonuses or luxury client gifts, calculate your projected tax liability for the year. Move that "tax reserve" into a high-yield savings account now so it's out of sight and earning interest.

- **Gift Deductibility Limits**: Remember that the IRS limits the deduction for business gifts to $25 per person per year. If you're planning a "Power Move" by gifting high-end items to your best clients, know that anything above that $25 mark is a personal expense, not a business write-off.

Business Travel Strategy: The "Business Purpose" Test

Many professionals combine Q4 holiday travel with business meetings. While this is a smart way to offset travel costs, the IRS is particularly watchful of "mixed-purpose" trips. To ensure your flights and lodging are 100% deductible, you must meet the primary business purpose requirements.

How to Secure Your Deduction:

1. The "Work Day" Ratio: For domestic travel, the trip must be primarily for business. A good rule of thumb is to ensure more than half of your days on the trip are "business days" (meetings, conferences, or site visits).
2. Document the "Why": The IRS requires you to prove the time, place, and business purpose. Keep a simple log or calendar invite that lists:
   - Who you met with.
   - What business was discussed.
   - How the meeting benefits your future income.

3. The 2025 Mileage Rate: If you are driving for business this holiday season, the standard mileage rate is 70 cents per mile. Keeping a digital mileage log now is much easier than trying to recreate one from memory in March.

Conclusion: The Final Sprint

As we close out Q3, the "Final Sprint" has officially begun. The moves you make in September are the difference between a stressful tax season and a victory lap in April. By securing your September 15th safety net, maxing out your retirement vehicles, and shielding your assets with strategic insurance, you aren't just following a plan—you're executing a Power Move.

Your Q3 Action Checklist:

- Deadline Check: Confirm if you owe a Q3 Estimated Payment or if your S-Corp extension is due by September 15th.
- Contribution Audit: Log into your 401(k) portal and ensure you'll hit the $23,500 (or $31,000+) limit by December 31st.
- Backdoor Roth: If you're a high-earner, start the conversion paperwork now to avoid year-end processing delays.
- HSA/Insurance Review: Prepare for Open Enrollment by selecting an HSA-eligible plan to capture that "Triple Tax Advantage."

| **46** |

OCTOBER: REAL ESTATE STRATEGIES

The $40,000 SALT Breakout

For nearly a decade, homeowners in high-tax states felt like they were shouting into a void. The 2017 Tax Cuts and Jobs Act (TCJA) introduced a "cap" on the State and Local Tax (SALT) deduction, limiting it to just $10,000. Whether you paid $15,000 or $50,000 in property and state income taxes, the IRS only let you write off that first ten thousand.

But as of January 1, 2025, the landscape has shifted. Under the One Big Beautiful Bill Act (OBBBA), signed into law on July 4, 2025, the SALT cap hasn't just been adjusted—it has been quadrupled.

The End of the $10,000 Cap

The OBBBA effectively ends the era of the "tax penalty" for living in high-value real estate markets. For the 2025 tax year, the

SALT deduction limit has been raised to $40,000 for single and joint filers earning under $500,000 in Modified Adjusted Gross Income (MAGI).

This isn't just a minor tweak; it's a restoration of your home's status as a primary tax-saving vehicle. If you live in a state like New Jersey, California, New York, or Illinois—where property taxes alone can easily consume that old $10,000 limit—this change could represent a massive reduction in your taxable income.

Key Rule for 2025: The $40,000 cap will increase by 1% annually through 2029, meaning the window for these high deductions is open for the foreseeable future, though it is currently set to revert to $10,000 in 2030.

Who Wins Most: The "Sweet Spot" Homeowner

While the "ultra-wealthy" are often the focus of tax talk, the OBBBA's SALT breakout is specifically designed for the upper-middle-class homeowner. To maximize this benefit, you generally need to fall into the "Sweet Spot":

- **Income Range**: Households with a MAGI between $150,000 and $500,000.
- **The Phaseout**: If your income exceeds $500,000, the deduction begins to "phase out" (reducing by 30 cents for every dollar over the limit). Once your income hits $600,000, the deduction reverts back to the old $10,000 floor.
- **Location**: Homeowners in high-property-tax counties who previously saw no tax benefit for their school and municipal tax payments.

The Itemization Shift: Is the Standard Deduction Dead?

Since 2018, nearly 90% of taxpayers stopped "itemizing" because the Standard Deduction was so high and the SALT cap was so low. It was simply easier to take the flat rate.

In 2025, that math has changed. Even though the Standard Deduction has risen to $31,500 for joint filers, many clients will find that their total itemized deductions—consisting of the new $40,000 SALT limit, mortgage interest, and charitable giving—will far exceed that amount.

Example Comparison (Joint Filers):

Category	2024 Strategy (Standard)	2025 Strategy (Itemized)
SALT Deduction	$10,000 (Capped)	$40,000
Mortgage Interest	$15,000	$15,000
Total Deduction	$29,200 (Standard)	**$55,000** (Itemized)
Tax Savings	Baseline	Approx. $6,000 - $9,000 more

As we move into the final weeks of the year, your goal should be to gather your property tax assessments and state income tax projections. If you've taken the standard deduction for the last seven years, prepare to switch gears.

| 47 |

MORTGAGE INTEREST & THE $750K RULE

M ortgage Debt

While the SALT breakout in Chapter 46 provides a significant boost, the other half of the itemization equation is your mortgage interest. For years, homeowners faced uncertainty about whether the lower debt limits introduced in 2017 would "sunset" and return to the old $1 million threshold.

The One Big Beautiful Bill Act (OBBBA) has finally provided an answer, bringing much-needed stability to long-term financial planning.

Permanence at Last: The $750,000 Debt Limit

The OBBBA has made the $750,000 mortgage debt limit permanent. This means that for any mortgage originated after December 15, 2017, you can deduct the interest paid on up to

$750,000 of "acquisition indebtedness" ($375,000 if married filing separately).

If your combined mortgage debt across your primary and secondary residence exceeds this amount, you don't lose the deduction entirely—you simply prorate it.

The "Grandfather" Reminder: If you have a mortgage that was originated on or before December 15, 2017, you are still "grandfathered" under the old $1 million limit. Even if you refinance that loan in 2025, you can generally maintain that $1 million threshold as long as the new principal doesn't exceed the old balance.

Second Homes: The "Qualified Residence" Advantage

One of the most powerful tools in the real estate tax toolkit is the ability to deduct interest on a second home. Under the 2025 rules, a "qualified residence" can be a house, condo, boat, or even a mobile home, provided it has basic sleeping, cooking, and toilet facilities.

To keep the interest deductible in 2025, you must follow the 14-Day/10% Rule:

- **Personal Use**: You must use the home personally for more than 14 days or 10% of the days it is rented out, whichever is greater.
- **Rental Strategy**: If you rent it out but stay within these limits, it remains a "residence," and the interest stays on your Schedule A. If you rent it out full-time and rarely visit, it shifts to a "business property," moving the interest deduc-

tion to Schedule E (which has different, often more restrictive, rules for passive losses).

The HELOC Trap: "Buy, Build, or Improve"

Many homeowners mistakenly believe all interest on a Home Equity Line of Credit (HELOC) is deductible because it is secured by their home. In 2025, the IRS remains strict: interest is only deductible if the funds were used to "buy, build, or substantially improve" the home that secures the loan.

- **Deductible**: Using a $50,000 HELOC to add a sunroom or remodel a kitchen.
- **NOT Deductible**: Using that same $50,000 to pay off credit card debt, buy a car, or fund a child's tuition.

As you look toward your April filing, ensure you have a "paper trail" (invoices and bank transfers) showing exactly where your HELOC draws went. Under the OBBBA, the IRS has increased audit resources for "mixed-use" loans, making this documentation more critical than ever.

| **48** |

THE INVESTOR'S EDGE

100% Bonus Depreciation

If Chapter 46 and 47 were about saving money on the home you live in, Chapter 48 is about the fuel that powers your real estate investment portfolio. For the past two years, investors watched nervously as "Bonus Depreciation"—the ability to write off large portions of a property's cost immediately—began to phase out, dropping to 60% in 2024 and scheduled to hit 40% in 2025.

The One Big Beautiful Bill Act (OBBBA) changed the game entirely. As of January 20, 2025, 100% Bonus Depreciation is back, and this time, it's permanent.

The Reinstatement: No More Phasedowns

The OBBBA has struck the old "phasedown" schedule from the tax code. This means that for any qualified property acquired and placed in service after January 19, 2025, you can once again deduct 100% of the cost in the very first year.

This is a massive win for cash flow. Instead of waiting decades to recover your investment through standard depreciation, you can "front-load" those deductions to wipe out taxable rental income—or even other types of income if you qualify as a Real Estate Professional.

Cost Segregation: The Secret to the 100% Write-Off

You might be wondering: "How can I write off a building in one year if the IRS says residential property must be depreciated over 27.5 years?" The answer is Cost Segregation.

A cost segregation study "unbundles" your property. While the "bricks and mortar" (the structure) still depreciate over 27.5 or 39 years, a specialized engineering report identifies components that are considered "personal property" or "land improvements." Under the OBBBA, these specific categories qualify for the 100% bonus:

- **5-Year Property**: Carpeting, specialty lighting, appliances, and cabinetry.
- **7-Year Property**: Office furniture and certain equipment.
- **15-Year Property**: Landscaping, fences, and paved parking lots.

By reclassifying 20% to 30% of your purchase price into these categories, you can generate a massive tax loss in Year 1 without ever actually "losing" a dime of cash.

The S-Corp & Pass-Through Advantage

For many of my clients who operate their real estate through S-Corps or LLCs, the OBBBA has also made the Section 199A (Qualified Business Income) deduction permanent. This allows you to deduct up to 20% of your qualified business income on top of your depreciation.

Furthermore, if you are a "Real Estate Professional" for tax purposes, the losses generated by 100% Bonus Depreciation aren't just limited to your rental income—they can be used to offset your active income (like W-2 wages or business profits). This remains one of the most powerful legal "tax shelters" available in the 2025 landscape.

| 49 |

THE LAST CALL FOR ENERGY CREDITS

Energy Credit Phase Out

If you've been procrastinating on that solar project or HVAC upgrade, the clock has officially started its final countdown. While previous legislation suggested these credits would last well into the 2030s, the One Big Beautiful Bill Act (OBBBA) has moved the finish line significantly closer.

For the American homeowner, 2025 is not just another year of eligibility—it is the "Sunset Year."

The 2025 Sunset: A Hard Deadline

The OBBBA has accelerated the expiration of the two most popular residential energy incentives. Unlike previous "phase-downs" where the percentage simply decreased, the OBBBA implements a hard stop:

- **Section 25C (Energy Efficient Home Improvement Credit)**: Terminated for all property placed in service after December 31, 2025.
- **Section 25D (Residential Clean Energy Credit)**: Terminated for all expenditures made after December 31, 2025.

This means if your solar panels are sitting in a crate on your driveway on New Year's Eve, you may be out of luck. To qualify, systems must be installed and operational before the ball drops.

The $3,200 Annual Limit: Maximize Every Dollar

Even with the looming deadline, the 2025 benefit remains robust. You can claim 30% of the cost of qualified upgrades, but the IRS applies a specific "bucket" system for the annual maximums:

1. **The $1,200 General Bucket**: This covers "building envelope" improvements like windows (capped at $600), exterior doors ($250 per door, $500 max), and home energy audits ($150).
2. **The $2,000 Heat Pump Bucket**: A separate limit applies specifically to electric or natural gas heat pumps, heat pump water heaters, and biomass stoves.
3. **The Total**: By combining these, a homeowner can effectively claim a $3,200 total tax credit in 2025.

Strategy Tip: Because these are annual limits, if you have multiple projects, the OBBBA's mid-year enactment makes it vital to ensure all 2025 projects are finalized by year-end, as there will be no "General Bucket" available in 2026.

The "Qualified Manufacturer" Rule

New for 2025 is a strict compliance hurdle: the QM Code. For an upgrade to qualify for the Section 25C credit this year, the item must be produced by a Qualified Manufacturer who has registered with the IRS.

When you purchase a central A/C unit, water heater, or heat pump this year, you must obtain a four-character alphanumeric QM Code (or a unique Product Identification Number) from the installer. You will be required to enter this code directly onto Form 5695 when you file your 2025 taxes. Without this code, the IRS computers are programmed to automatically reject the credit.

Residential Clean Energy (Solar & Battery)

While the $3,200 limit applies to "improvements," the Residential Clean Energy Credit (Section 25D) for solar, wind, and battery storage still has no dollar limit. You get a straight 30% credit on the entire cost.

However, since this credit is also set to vanish at the end of 2025, the demand for installers is expected to peak in October and November. If you are considering solar or a whole-home battery backup, the "Last Call" isn't just a marketing slogan—it's a tax reality.

| 50 |

SELLING & INHERITING

The $15M Shield

As we reach the final stage of the property lifecycle—selling or passing it on to the next generation—the One Big Beautiful Bill Act (OBBBA) has introduced what many are calling the most generous wealth transfer environment in American history. By stabilizing the rules and dramatically raising the stakes, the 2025 laws have effectively created a "shield" around your real estate equity.

The Capital Gains Exclusion: Section 121

Before we look at inheritance, let's look at the exit strategy for your primary home. The OBBBA preserved the Section 121 Exclusion, which remains one of the greatest tax gifts in the code.

If you have owned and lived in your home for at least two out of the last five years, you can exclude up to $250,000 (single) or $500,000 (married filing jointly) of profit from capital gains tax. In a 2025 market where home values have surged, this exclusion is the difference between keeping your full check at closing or handing a massive chunk to the IRS.

Pro Tip: The two years do not have to be consecutive. If you lived in the home for one year, rented it for two, and moved back for one final year before selling, you still qualify for the full exclusion.

The $15 Million Estate Baseline

The headline news of the OBBBA is the permanent increase of the federal estate tax exemption. Starting January 1, 2026 (based on the 2025 legislative reset), the individual exemption will rise to $15 million per person.

For a married couple, this creates a $30 million shield.

Previously, families were panicking that the exemption would "sunset" and drop to $7 million. The OBBBA removed that "ticking clock," giving you the peace of mind to hold onto high-value real estate without the fear that your children will be forced to sell the family home or farm just to pay an estate tax bill.

The Power of the "Step-Up in Basis"

While the $15 million exemption is impressive, the real "real estate reward" is the preservation of the Step-Up in Basis.

When you sell a property during your lifetime, you pay taxes on the growth from the day you bought it (the "basis"). However, if you pass that property to an heir at your death, their new tax basis is the fair market value on the day you passed away.

The 2025 Math:

- **Original Purchase Price (1995):** $200,000
- **Market Value at Death (2025):** $2,200,000
- **The Reward**: Your heirs can sell the property for $2.2 million immediately and pay $0 in capital gains tax. They effectively "wipe out" $2 million in taxable appreciation.

By combining the new $15 million exemption with the Step-Up in Basis, the OBBBA has ensured that real estate remains the premier vehicle for building—and keeping—multi-generational wealth.

CONCLUSION & CALL TO ACTION (CTA)

The "Property Tax Revolution" of 2025 has turned the old rules upside down. From the quadrupled SALT cap to the return of 100% bonus depreciation, the window for maximizing your real estate benefits is wider than it has been in a decade. But windows eventually close, and the best tax strategies are those implemented before the year-end.

- Cost Segregation Analysis: Thinking of buying an investment property before December 31st? Let's run a cost-segregation projection to see how much of that purchase price we can wipe out in Year 1.
- SALT Cap Review: Let's look at your projected property and state income taxes. If you're over the old $10k limit but under $40k, it's time to move back to itemizing and claim your refund.

NOVEMBER: THE ART OF GIVING

Giving: Itemized Deductions

For decades, the math of charitable giving was relatively straightforward: if you itemized your deductions, every dollar you gave to a qualified charity reduced your taxable income. However, the legislative landscape has shifted. With the passage of the One Big Beautiful Bill Act (OBBBA), the rules of the game are changing significantly starting January 1, 2026.

If you are a high-income earner or a consistent donor, 2025 represents a "golden window" of opportunity. After this year, the tax code introduces new hurdles that will make it harder—and more expensive—to claim the same benefits you enjoy today.

The New 0.5% Rule: Understanding the "Floor"

Starting in 2026, the government is introducing what tax professionals call a deduction floor. For those who itemize, charitable contributions will only be deductible to the extent that they exceed 0.5% of your Adjusted Gross Income (AGI).

Think of this as a "deductible" on your insurance policy. You have to pay the first bit out of pocket before the benefits kick in.

Example: If your household AGI is $200,000, your "charity floor" is $1,000 ($200,000 x 0.005).

- **In 2025**: A $1,000 gift is fully deductible.
- **In 2026**: A $1,000 gift results in $0 in itemized deductions. You must give $1,001 to see your first penny of tax benefit.

For many families, this floor effectively wipes out the tax benefit of their "baseline" annual giving—the smaller, consistent gifts to local shelters, schools, or houses of worship.

The 35% Benefit Cap: A Warning for High Earners

If you are in the top marginal tax bracket (currently 37%), your charitable gifts have historically been a powerful lever to reduce your tax bill. In 2025, a $10,000 gift can save you $3,700 in federal taxes.

However, the OBBBA introduces a "cap" on the value of these deductions. Starting in 2026, the tax benefit for itemized deductions—including charitable gifts—will be limited to 35%, regardless of whether you are in the 37% bracket.

- **2025 Value**: $0.37 tax savings per $1 donated.
- **2026 Value**: $0.35 tax savings per $1 donated.

While a 2% difference might seem small, for a donor gifting $50,000 or $100,000, that's thousands of dollars in lost tax efficiency.

The 2025 Advantage: December 31 vs. January 1

The "Giving Cliff" is real. Because of the combination of the new 0.5% floor and the 35% benefit cap, a gift made on December 31, 2025, is mathematically superior to the exact same gift made on January 1, 2026.

By acting before the clock strikes midnight on New Year's Eve, you avoid the floor entirely and lock in the higher 37% deduction rate. In the next chapter, we'll discuss how you can use "Bunching" to take advantage of these 2025 rules even if you aren't ready to choose your specific charities yet.

| **52** |

THE DONOR-ADVISED FUND (DAF) "BUNCHING" STRATEGY

Donation Solutions

As we saw in Chapter 51, the 2026 "Charity Floor" and the deduction cap are set to make your giving less tax-efficient. If you typically donate a consistent amount each year, you might find yourself losing out on thousands of dollars in potential tax savings.

The solution? Bunching.

Locking in 2025 Benefits

"Bunching" is a strategy where you concentrate several years of planned charitable giving into a single tax year. By making one large contribution in 2025, you bypass the upcoming 2026 floor and secure your deduction at the current higher tax rates.

For most people, the challenge is that they don't want to give away three years of support to their favorite nonprofit all at once—perhaps they want to ensure the charity has a steady stream of income, or they haven't decided which organizations to support in 2027 or 2028.

This is where the Donor-Advised Fund (DAF) becomes your most powerful tool.

The Immediate Win: Pay Yourself a "Tax Refund" Now

When you contribute to a DAF, the IRS treats it as a completed gift to a public charity. This means you get the full tax deduction immediately in 2025, even if the money sits in the fund for years.

- **No 0.5% Floor**: Because you are giving in 2025, every dollar (up to AGI limits) is eligible for deduction without the "0.5% deductible" that starts in 2026.
- **37% Deduction Value**: If you are in the top bracket, you save $0.37 on the dollar, rather than the $0.35 you would receive if you waited until 2026.
- **Tax-Free Growth**: Once the money is in your DAF, it can be invested. Any growth is tax-free, meaning your $50,000 contribution today could become $60,000 of impact for your charities tomorrow.

Flexibility: Give When You're Ready

The beauty of the DAF is the separation of the tax event from the charitable act.

1. **Fund it in 2025**: You write the check or transfer the stock to the DAF by December 31st to secure your 2025 tax break.
2. **Grant over time**: In 2026, 2027, and beyond, you log into your DAF portal and recommend "grants" to your local food bank, alma mater, or house of worship.

The charities receive their support exactly when they need it, but you've already "pre-paid" your giving during the most tax-advantaged year possible.

Strategic Note: This is especially effective if 2025 is a high-income year for you—perhaps due to a business sale, a large bonus, or a Roth IRA conversion. A DAF allows you to offset that high income when it matters most.

QUALIFIED CHARITABLE DISTRIBUTIONS (QCDS) FOR SENI

Traditional Giving Tax Benefit Challenge

As we move into 2026, many of the traditional tax benefits for charitable giving will be squeezed by new "floors" and "caps." However, for those aged 70½ or older, there is a strategy that bypasses these new restrictions entirely. It is arguably the most efficient way to give in the current tax environment: the Qualified Charitable Distribution (QCD).

The Direct Transfer: Simple and Powerful

A QCD is a direct transfer of funds from your IRA custodian to a qualified 501(c)(3) charity. Because the money never touches your personal bank account, the IRS does not count it as taxable income.

In 2025, the annual limit for QCDs is $108,000 per person. If you are married, both you and your spouse can each contribute up to this amount from your respective IRAs, for a total of $216,000 in tax-free giving.

The RMD Shield: Keeping Your Income "Lean"

For many retirees, the biggest tax headache is the Required Minimum Distribution (RMD). Once you reach age 73 (or 75 if you were born in 1960 or later), the government forces you to take money out of your IRA—and pay ordinary income tax on every dollar.

The QCD acts as a shield. By directing your RMD (or a portion of it) to a charity, you satisfy your legal requirement to withdraw the money, but you exclude the amount from your Adjusted Gross Income (AGI). This has a massive ripple effect on your overall finances:

- **Lower Social Security Taxation**: Since your AGI is lower, less of your Social Security benefit may be subject to tax.
- **Medicare Premium Savings**: Medicare Part B and D premiums are often based on your income from two years prior (a surcharge known as IRMAA). By using a QCD to keep your income below certain thresholds, you can save thousands in future healthcare costs.
- **Avoiding "Bracket Creep"**: Keeping RMD income off your return helps prevent you from being pushed into a higher tax bracket.

The "Non-Itemizer Hack"

Under the new rules of the One Big Beautiful Bill Act (OBBBA), the vast majority of Americans take the standard deduction rather than itemizing. Normally, this means you get zero tax benefit for your charitable gifts.

The QCD is the ultimate loophole. Because a QCD reduces your income before you even look at deductions, you effectively get the tax benefit of your gift on top of the standard deduction.

Comparison for a $10,000 Gift:

- **The Cash Giver**: Takes the standard deduction. The $10,000 gift provides no additional tax savings.
- **The QCD Giver**: Takes the standard deduction AND excludes $10,000 from their taxable income. At a 24% tax rate, they just saved $2,400 in taxes that the cash giver had to pay.

As we approach the 2026 "Charity Floor," the QCD remains one of the only ways to ensure your first dollar of giving is 100% tax-efficient.

| **54** |

BEYOND CASH

GIFTING APPRECIATED STOCK

When most people think of charity, they think of their checkbook. But if you have an investment portfolio, writing a check is often the least efficient way to give. If you own stocks, mutual funds, or ETFs that have grown in value, you are sitting on a powerful tax-saving tool.

As we move toward the 2026 "Charity Floor," maximizing every dollar becomes even more critical. In 2025, the rule remains: Never give cash if you have winning stocks.

The Double Tax Benefit

Donating "appreciated" securities (assets held for more than one year that have increased in value) creates a "double win" that cash simply cannot match.

177

1. **Avoid the Gains**: When you sell a winning stock, you typically owe up to 23.8% in federal capital gains taxes (including the Medicare surtax). By donating the stock directly, that tax disappears. Neither you nor the charity pays it.
2. **Full Market Value Deduction**: Even though you never paid taxes on the growth, the IRS allows you to deduct the full fair market value of the stock on the day you give it.

Pro Tip: If you love the stock and don't want to lose your position, donate the "old" shares to charity and use your "new" cash to buy the same stock back immediately. You've now "reset" your cost basis to today's high price, drastically reducing your future tax bill if you ever sell.

The Rebalancing Move: "Cleaning Up" Your Portfolio

By November or December, many investors realize their portfolio has become "top-heavy" in certain winners. Perhaps a tech stock that was once 10% of your holdings is now 20%. Selling those shares to rebalance would normally trigger a massive tax bill.

Donating is the ultimate rebalancing hack. Instead of selling your winners and paying the IRS, you "trim" your over-concentrated positions by gifting them to your Donor-Advised Fund or favorite charity.

- You restore your target asset allocation.
- You eliminate the concentrated risk in your portfolio.
- You secure a massive 2025 tax deduction before the 2026 rules kick in.

Crucial Timing: The 30% Limit

While cash donations can generally be deducted up to 60% of your Adjusted Gross Income (AGI), gifts of appreciated stock are capped at 30% of your AGI.

If you are planning a very large gift in 2025—perhaps to "bunch" several years of giving before the 2026 cliff—we need to run the numbers to ensure you don't exceed this limit. Any excess can be carried forward for five years, but remember: those future deductions will be subject to the 2026 Charity Floor and the 35% Benefit Cap.

| 55 |

THE UNIVERSAL DEDUCTION
FOR EVERYONE

Itemizing Help

While much of the recent tax news focuses on high-income earn-ers and the "giving cliff," there is a significant silver lining for the nearly 90% of Americans who take the standard deduction. Thanks to the One Big Beautiful Bill Act (OBBBA), a permanent tax benefit for "everyday" giving has been restored and expanded.

The $1,000/$2,000 Win

For years, if you didn't itemize, your charitable gifts didn't pro-vide any direct tax relief. The OBBBA changes that by introducing a permanent "above-the-line" deduction. This means you can sub-tract your charitable gifts from your gross income before the stan-dard deduction is even applied.

- **Single Filers**: Can deduct up to $1,000 in cash gifts.
- **Married Filing Jointly**: Can deduct up to $2,000 in cash gifts.

Starting in 2026, this "universal" deduction allows you to lower your taxable income even if you take the newly increased standard deduction (which sits at $31,500 for married couples in 2025). This ensures that smaller, consistent gifts to local charities still carry a tangible tax reward.

Note of Caution: This specific deduction only applies to cash gifts (checks, credit cards, or wire transfers) made directly to operating public charities. Gifts to Donor-Advised Funds (DAFs) or private foundations do not qualify for this above-the-line benefit.

Documentation is King

Even with the new universal deduction, the IRS hasn't relaxed its record-keeping requirements. To claim any charitable deduction—whether you itemize or use the new $1,000/$2,000 provision—you must be prepared to prove it.

- **The $250 Rule**: For any single gift of $250 or more, a simple bank statement or cancelled check is not enough. You must have a Contemporaneous Written Acknowledgment (CWA) from the charity. This letter must state the amount given and confirm whether you received any goods or services in exchange for the gift.
- **Year-End Timing**: A gift is considered "made" the day it is mailed or processed. If you are aiming for a 2025 deduction, ensure your checks are postmarked or your online credit card transactions are completed by December 31st.

CONCLUSION: YOUR 2025 ACTION PLAN

The transition from 2025 to 2026 represents one of the most significant shifts in the history of American philanthropy. With the 0.5% floor and the 35% benefit cap looming, waiting until next year to give will literally cost you money.

Strategic philanthropy isn't just about how much you give—it's about how and when you give. By taking action before December 31, 2025, you can ensure that more of your wealth goes to the causes you love and less goes to the IRS.

Next Steps: How We Can Help

Don't navigate the "Giving Cliff" alone. We are here to help you maximize your impact before the window closes.

- **The "Giving Goal" Consultation**: Let's sit down and look at your projected 2025 income. We can run the numbers to see if a year-end "Bunching" strategy can save you thousands in taxes before the new floor kicks in.
- **DAF Setup & Funding**: If you want to lock in your 2025 tax benefits but aren't ready to choose your specific charities yet, we can help you open and fund a Donor-Advised Fund in time for the December 31st deadline.
- **Stock Transfer Audit**: We can review your portfolio for highly appreciated assets that are ripe for donation, allowing you to avoid capital gains tax while making a major impact.

The clock is ticking on the most favorable giving environment we've seen in years. Contact our office today to schedule your Year-End Giving Review.

| **56** |

DECEMBER: THE YEAR-END COUNTDOWN

THE "NEW DEDUCTION" TRIPLE THREAT

The 2025 tax landscape isn't just different—it's been completely reshaped. With the passing of the One Big Beautiful Bill Act (OBBBA) in July, the IRS isn't just looking for what you earned; it's offering a series of massive, time-sensitive "wins" that specifically reward service workers, seniors, and buyers of American-made goods.

However, there is a catch: these are not "automatic" credits. To claim your share of these three major OBBBA victories, you must understand the rules and act before the ball drops on December 31st.

1. Overtime & Tips: The Service Industry Revolution

For years, tipped employees and hourly workers have felt the heavy hand of the IRS on their extra effort. The OBBBA has flipped the script. Starting in 2025, the "premium" portion of your hard work is now shielded from federal income tax.

- **The Overtime Break**: If you are a non-exempt employee, you can now deduct the "premium" portion of your overtime pay (the extra 0.5x in "time-and-a-half") up to $12,500 annually ($25,000 for joint filers).
- **The Tip Exemption**: Service industry professionals can deduct up to $25,000 in qualified tips.
- **The Deadline Rule**: Because 2025 is a transition year, W-2 forms may not show these amounts in a separate box yet. You must keep meticulous logs of your overtime hours and tip reports from now until December 31st to substantiate this deduction.

2. The Senior Bonus: A $6,000 "Thank You"

If you are 65 or older by December 31st, 2025, the OBBBA has introduced what many are calling the "Senior Bonus." This is a flat $6,000 deduction ($12,000 for married couples where both are 65+) that sits right on top of your standard or itemized deductions.

Watch the Phase-Out: This bonus is designed for the middle class. The deduction begins to disappear once your Modified

Adjusted Gross Income (MAGI) hits $75,000 (Single) or $150,000 (Joint). If you are near these limits, December is the time to defer income or harvest losses to stay below the threshold and keep your full $6,000 bonus.

3. Auto Loan Interest: Buying American Pays Off

In a move to bolster U.S. manufacturing, the OBBBA now allows you to deduct the interest on auto loans for vehicles assembled in the United States.

- **No Itemization Required**: This is an "above-the-line" deduction, meaning you get it even if you take the standard deduction.
- **The Limits**: You can deduct up to $10,000 in interest paid in 2025.
- **Verification**: The vehicle must be new (purchased in 2025) and personal-use. To claim it, you'll need to provide your

VIN on your tax return. Check your VIN today; if it starts with a 1, 4, or 5, it was likely assembled in the U.S. and qualifies for this major 11th-hour saving.

THE INVESTMENT HARVEST

Turning Market Loosers into Tax Winners

The end of the year is often seen as a time for celebration, but for the savvy investor, it is a time for strategic pruning. With the stock market's volatility in late 2025 and the massive mid-year shift brought by the One Big Beautiful Bill Act (OBBBA), your portfolio likely contains hidden opportunities to lower your tax bill.

In this chapter, we focus on turning market "losers" into tax "winners" and using the OBBBA's permanent new incentives to fund your business growth.

1. Tax-Loss Harvesting: Offsetting the Wins

If you've sold stocks, ETFs, or mutual funds at a gain this year, you're looking at a potential capital gains tax hit. Tax-loss harvesting is the process of selling underperforming assets to neutralize those gains.

- **Dollar-for-Dollar Offset**: You can use $1 of loss to cancel out $1 of gain. If your losses exceed your gains, you can use up to $3,000 of the excess to offset your ordinary income (wages, interest, etc.).
- **The 2025 Rollover**: Any loss beyond that $3,000 doesn't disappear; it "rolls over" to 2026 and beyond, providing a future tax shield.
- **Beware the Wash-Sale Rule**: You cannot sell a stock for a loss and buy it (or something "substantially identical") back within 30 days before or after the sale. If you do, the IRS will disallow the loss.

2. The OBBBA 100% Bonus Depreciation: A Business "Must-Act"

Before the OBBBA, bonus depreciation was scheduled to drop to 40% in 2025. The new law didn't just stop the decline—it permanently restored 100% bonus depreciation for qualifying property acquired and placed in service after January 19, 2025.

- What Qualifies? Equipment, machinery, computers, software, and even certain "qualified production property" (like manufacturing facilities) are eligible.
- **The Deadline**: To write off the full cost of an asset in 2025, it must be "placed in service" by midnight on December 31st. "Placed in service" means the equipment is not just purchased, but is physically at your business and ready to be used.
- **Section 179 Expansion**: The OBBBA also boosted Section 179 limits to $2.5 million, giving you even more flexibility to choose which deduction method best suits your cash flow needs.

3. Crypto Review: The New "1009-DA" Reality

For years, the IRS treated crypto with a "soft touch." That era ended on January 1, 2025. This year marks the first time digital asset brokers are required to track and report your transactions to the IRS using the new Form 1099-DA.

- **Wallet-by-Wallet Accounting**: Starting this year, the IRS requires you to use a "wallet-by-wallet" method for cost basis rather than a universal average across all your holdings.
- **Document Everything**: Even if you don't receive your 1099-DA until early 2026, the IRS expects you to have documented the fair market value of every trade, swap, and "airdrop" received in 2025.
- **Clean Up Now**: Use December to reconcile your digital wallets. If you have "dead" coins that have lost all value, selling or disposing of them before year-end can provide a valuable capital loss to offset your other 2025 gains.

| 58 |

RETIREMENT & ROTH CONVERSIONS

From a Traditional to Roth Conversion

As the year winds down, most people are focused on holiday shopping, but your most valuable "gift" might be the one you give to your future self. 2025 has brought significant changes to how much you can squirrel away for retirement. With the One Big Beautiful Bill Act (OBBBA) now in full effect alongside the SECURE 2.0 provisions, the "standard" advice you heard last year is officially outdated.

1. The 401(k) Max-Out: New 2025 Limits

The IRS has increased the contribution limits for workplace retirement plans (401(k), 403(b), and most 457 plans). If you haven't adjusted your payroll deferrals lately, you might fall short of the new maximums.

- **Under Age 50**: You can now contribute up to $23,500.
- **Age 50+**: You are eligible for a "Catch-Up" contribution of an additional $7,500, bringing your total potential deferral to $31,000.
- **The "All-In" Limit**: If your employer offers matching or profit-sharing, the total combined limit (employee + employer) has jumped to $70,000 for 2025 ($77,500 for those 50+).

2. The "Super Catch-Up": A 2025 Exclusive

This is the "crown jewel" of the new retirement rules. Starting this year, a specific group of savers gets a massive boost.

- **Who Qualifies**: If you turn 60, 61, 62, or 63 by December 31, 2025.
- **The Bonus**: Instead of the standard $7,500 catch-up, you are eligible for the Super Catch-Up of $11,250.
- **The Total**: This allows you to put away a staggering $34,750 into your workplace plan this year.
- **The "Wait" Rule**: Note that once you turn 64, your catch-up limit actually reverts back to the standard amount. This 4-year window is a high-speed lane for retirement savings—don't let December pass without checking if your HR department has enabled this new "Super" tier.

3. The Roth Conversion Window

A Roth conversion—moving money from a Traditional IRA to a Roth IRA—is a "pay now, save later" strategy. Because you pay taxes on the converted amount today, the money grows tax-free forever.

- Why 2025? If 2025 was a lower-income year for you (perhaps due to a career change, business loss, or retirement), you may be in a lower tax bracket than usual. Converting now allows you to "lock in" these lower rates.
- **The OBBBA Edge**: With the new OBBBA deductions mentioned in Chapter 1 (like the Senior Bonus or Overtime deductions) lowering your overall taxable income, you might find you have "room" in your current tax bracket to convert $10k, $20k, or $50k without being pushed into a higher tier.
- **No "Take-Backs"**: Remember, once you convert to a Roth, you cannot "recharacterize" (undo) it. You must have the conversion completed by December 31st to count for the 2025 tax year.

59

THE 2026 GIVING CLIFF PREPARATION

Preparing to Give

For decades, the math of charitable giving was simple: if you itemized, every dollar you gave reduced your taxable income. But the One Big Beautiful Bill Act (OBBBA) has introduced a major structural change that takes effect on January 1, 2026. This creates a "Giving Cliff" that makes your 2025 year-end donations more valuable than those you make just a few weeks later in January.

1. Beat the Floor: The 0.5% AGI Hurdle

Starting in 2026, the OBBBA introduces a "floor" for charitable deductions. If you itemize, you will only be able to deduct gifts that exceed 0.5% of your Adjusted Gross Income (AGI).

- The Math: If your AGI is $200,000, the first $1,000 of your donations in 2026 will provide zero tax benefit. If your AGI is $1,000,000, that floor jumps to $5,000.

- Why 2025 is Better: In 2025, there is no floor. Every dollar you give—from the very first dollar—is potentially deductible if you itemize. By accelerating your planned 2026 giving into December 2025, you bypass this "tax on giving" entirely.

2. "Bunching" into DAFs: Your Best 11th-Hour Move

If you want to beat the 2026 Giving Cliff but aren't sure which charities you want to support yet, a Donor-Advised Fund (DAF) is your secret weapon.

- How It Works: You make a large contribution to a DAF before December 31st. You receive the full tax deduction in 2025 at the more generous "no-floor" rules.
- The Flexibility: The money sits in the fund (and can even be invested to grow tax-free). You can then "grant" that money to your favorite local charities over the next two or three years.
- The Strategy: This "bunching" strategy allows you to clear the standard deduction hurdle in 2025 and avoid the 0.5% floor in 2026, all while maintaining your regular level of support for your community.

3. The $115,000 QCD Deadline

For those 70½ or older, the Qualified Charitable Distribution (QCD) remains the most efficient way to give. It allows you to send money directly from your IRA to a charity without it ever showing up as taxable income.

- The 2025 Limit: You can distribute up to $108,000 per person ($216,000 for a married couple).
- The 2026 Increase: While the OBBBA increases this limit to $115,000 in 2026, waiting might be a mistake if you have a Required Minimum Distribution (RMD) to satisfy for 2025.
- The December 31st Hard Stop: Unlike IRA contributions (which can sometimes be made up until April), a QCD must leave your account by December 31st. If the check hasn't cleared or the wire hasn't been processed by year-end, it counts toward your 2026 limit instead, potentially leaving you with an under-distributed RMD for 2025 and a stiff penalty.

60

THE PAPERWORK CLEAN-UP

The Final Countdown

With only days remaining in 2025, it's easy to focus solely on the "big" deductions and miss the administrative housekeeping that ensures your savings actually reach your pocket. This year, "paperwork" isn't just about filing receipts—it's about adapting to a major technological shift in how the IRS communicates and pays out.

1. FSA "Use It or Lose It"

If you have a Flexible Spending Account (FSA), the clock is ticking. Unlike an HSA, most FSA funds expire at midnight on December 31st.

- **Check Your Balance**: Don't let your hard-earned money revert to your employer.
- **The "Stock Up" Strategy**: If you have remaining funds, remember that many over-the-counter items are now eligible. Stock up on first-aid supplies, sunscreens (SPF 15+), or

even high-tech items like smart thermometers or prescription sunglasses.

- **The Grace Period**: Check if your specific plan offers a 2.5-month grace period or a $640 carryover option. If it doesn't, you need to spend that balance now.

2. W-4 Review: The OBBBA Mid-Year Correction

Many taxpayers are in for a surprise in 2026—but not necessarily a bad one. Because the OBBBA cuts were implemented mid-year, many employers' payroll systems didn't fully adjust. This means you might have been "over-withholding" for the last six months.

- **The Holiday Bonus Hack**: By updating your W-4 for the final pay cycle of December, you can reduce your withholding and keep more of your last paycheck for holiday expenses.
- **Avoid the "Loan to Uncle Sam"**: If you're expecting a massive refund due to the new 2025 deductions, you are effectively giving the government an interest-free loan. Use the last few days of the year to align your withholding with the new OBBBA reality.

3. The 2026 "No-Paper-Check" Rule

Perhaps the most significant administrative shift in a generation occurred in March 2025, when President Trump signed

> Executive Order 14247. This mandate requires the IRS to phase out paper checks for federal disbursements by September 30, 2025.

- **What it Means for You**: For the 2025 tax returns you file in early 2026, the IRS is effectively eliminating paper refund checks.
- **The Speed Gap**: If you do not provide direct deposit information, the IRS has stated they may hold your refund for up to six weeks while they send letters requesting electronic payment details or processing limited hardship exceptions.
- **Action Item**: Don't wait for the filing season. Use December to ensure you have your routing and account numbers ready. If you are unbanked, now is the time to set up a digital wallet or a Treasury-approved prepaid card to ensure your 2025 refund isn't caught in "paperwork limbo."

CONCLUSION: THE "LAST CHANCE" STRATEGY SESSION

The OBBBA has made 2025 a landmark year for tax savings, but these benefits are only for those who cross the finish line before the midnight deadline on December 31st.

Whether it's claiming the "Senior Bonus," harvesting investment losses, or bypassing the 2026 "Giving Cliff," the window for action is closing.

The Year Isn't Over Yet. Don't leave your OBBBA credits on the table. Book a 20-minute "Final Look" session with our team this week. We will review your 2025 numbers and ensure you have locked in every possible deduction before the clock strikes twelve.

Looking Ahead: Once we've secured your 2025 savings, it's time to play offense for the future. Join our "New Year, New Wealth" webinar in January, where we will dive deep into the 2026 tax landscape and how to build on the momentum we've started here.